NATURE CRAFTS
for All the Seasons

Amber Cook

Sterling Publishing Co., Inc.
New York

Editor: Leslie Dierks
Art Director: Kathleen Holmes
Production: Elaine Thompson, Kathleen Holmes

Library of Congress Cataloging-in-Publication Data Available

10   9   8   7   6   5   4   3   2   1

Published by Sterling Publishing Company, Inc.
387 Park Avenue South, New York, NY 10016
Produced by Altamont Press, Inc.
50 College Street, Asheville, NC 28801
© 1993 by Amber Cook
Distributed in Canada by Sterling Publishing
% Canadian Manda Group, P.O. Box 920, Station U
Toronto, Ontario, Canada M8Z 5P9
Distributed in Great Britain and Europe by Cassell PLC
Villiers House, 41/47 Strand, London WC2N 5JE, England
Distributed in Australia by Capricorn Link Ltd.
P.O. Box 665, Lane Cove, NSW 2066
Printed and Bound in Hong Kong
All rights reserved

Sterling ISBN 0-8069-8602-6

Photo: Richard A. Brown

To Gayle, Steve, Jamie, Sandy, Scott, and Robin, with love.

CONTENTS

INTRODUCTION

Nature and crafts—there is something wonderfully adventurous about each. In this book we'll travel season by season, finding the roads that lead us on those exciting sojourns of exploration and discovery. Many of the projects are designed with children in mind, to make sure they experience, and never forget, what we adults have come to know about the ways of wildflowers and the wonders of marsh and woodland trails, meadows and seashore.

"Nature is our widest home," wrote Henry David Thoreau, who found a sweet sanctuary beneath the ancient oaks at Walden Pond. Coming home with a handful, pocketful, or armful of nature's treasures, we become aware of nature's bounty. Dried and handcrafted, they are like little presents from nature to be treasured again and again.

In a seasonal arrangement of the projects, you'll find twigs and branches gently crafted into a child's chair and tea table. Drifts of seashells from the ocean sands are nested in a waxy white wreath of twisted honeysuckle vines. Natural clay from the backyard and country road are molded into earth-colored pots. Pine needles that once carpeted the forest floor are shaped into tiny keepsake baskets. These are all reminders of the richness of nature's treasures that we can bring into our everyday lives.

We taste the excitement of spring treasures first, building rustic furniture and baskets from willow whips and other fresh, new growth of the season. Although colored eggs and Easter baskets are the province of children, we can all enjoy the process of creating those treasures for Easter dreams. Wool, the texture of spring's fairest hours, comes indoors where it is molded into the finest felt purses and cozy slippers. Honeysuckle vines are cleverly twined into a "natural" birdcage.

The second section is filled with the joys of nature that mark a summer's day. We can capture the beauty of herbs by framing them within beveled glass. A personal bookmark recalls the delicate beauty of pressed wildflowers, and rose petals are fashioned into beads for a sweet-scented necklace that will last forever. Comfortable summer sandals are crafted from natural fiber. Wearing these, you can stroll the beaches, collecting seashells to make a soothing wind chime. It is a world of quiet summer pleasures.

Next, the cooler autumn days bid farewell to fresh blooming roses and wildflowers. Now we dry the blossoms and collect branches full of berries to make welcoming wreaths. We come alive to autumn's palette, collecting colorful leaves to create our own mural in rich amber and russet shades. An assortment of chile peppers in fall colors of mustard yellow, bright red, and green hang in the kitchen to delight the eye as they dry, and cattails come indoors to become handsome decoys or tiny toy chairs. A world of fall pleasures awaits.

The fourth section is filled with nature's own designs for the winter months. Now we bundle up for a stroll in the woods to collect pine needles to make a lidded basket for candy or guest soaps, and, while we're there, to cut a handful of branches to make into a rustic, natural table lamp. Winter is a time to bridge the seasons, to pause over the spring, summer, and fall collections. The natural beauty of rice paper pillow sachets, a wreath made from dried apple slices, and a mirror framed in bay leaves of gold create keepsake treasures to be enjoyed all through winter and beyond.

Finally, in a chapter on the basics of nature crafts, you'll find a wide selection of helpful hints for making many of the projects in this book. It's a handy guide for those who want to brush up on basketry and other techniques, or for those who have yet to collect their first vine from the woods. Here you'll learn what to look for when you head out into the woods, and how to cure, strip, and maintain the suppleness of your materials. You'll be introduced to twining and different methods for finishing off a basket. And you'll learn how easy it is to make a professional-looking wreath.

Springtime brings with it a rush of excitement, the anticipation of new beginnings. As the days grow longer, the earth shrugs off the deep sleep of winter and sends forth tender new shoots and delicate blossoms.

Twig projects made from willow are especially well suited to early spring, before the leaves have fully formed and obscured the lines of the branches. A child's willow chair uses sturdy branches to provide a strong frame, and adds supple whips to reflect the freeform look of nature. Willow branches can be easily assembled into an elegant planter for your favorite potted plants. A glass-topped tea table evokes its forest origin, reminding us that nature is beautiful in its simplicity. Directions for making the chair begin on page 17, the basket is on page 22, and the tea table on page 20.

Making baskets for Easter is the perfect excuse for a walk in the woods to gather slender vines, bits of moss, and delicate flowers to dry. Be sure to collect plenty of flowers and small leaves to use as decorations for eggs that are colored with natural dyes made from vegetables, nuts, and berries. Instructions for the Easter basket can be found on page 32, and the natural dye is described on page 31.

What better way is there to take advantage of sheep-shearing time than by making felt? Soft, yet sturdy, your own homemade felt can be sewn into small purses that make perfect accessories, or into cozy slippers to warm the feet of someone you love. Directions start on page 29.

With warmer weather, familiar birds return to build nests and raise their young. You can translate the welcome rat-a-tat-tat of your neighborhood woodpecker into a child-pleasing door knocker. You only need a log, a few scraps of wood, a leather shoelace, and a bit of paint to make either the downy (right) or the hairy (below) woodpecker knocker. Directions begin on page 26. Entice your favorite bird to nest in your yard by building his house for him! This quaint house is made from honeysuckle vines, and the top can be removed for easy cleaning between seasons. See the instructions on page 37.

Honeysuckle vine is especially beautiful when stripped of its bark and coiled into a gentle heart shape. With a decoration of spring flowers and a colorful bow, this spring wreath makes a unique Valentine. Instructions are on page 25.

Whether it is filled with flowers, a live plant, or an artificial bird, this birdcage made with willow whips is an enchanting decoration for tabletop or étagère. Directions can be found on page 23.

Supple enough to shape into delicate baskets, willow reed is also strong enough to be child proof. Small-scale, open baskets are perfect for a child's Easter basket or for an artful display in your home. See page 34 for instructions.

Smooth, green cattail leaves make an interesting texture when dried and woven into a basket. You can vary the dimensions to fit a single, favorite plant, or make a graduated set of baskets to cluster in a sunny corner.

For thousands of years, nearly every culture has used native clay to make vessels for drinking, eating, and storage. Using clay from your back yard, and your fingers as tools, you can make an assortment of shapes that, when dried, can be painted to resemble primitive pottery.

Directions for the cattail basket start on page 27, and the clay vases begin on page 35.

Child's Willow Chair

see photo page 8

When you venture into the woods in search of the branches that will become your new chair, you are in for a magnificent surprise. You will begin to discover a new way of perceiving and organizing design, and for improvising with the interesting forms and shapes that nature offers in limbs, twigs, and roots.

Rustic work makes use of small trees, roots, and branches, and the design of each piece is enhanced by whimsy and an indifferent attitude to the measuring stick. The maker learns to rely on his eye, only casual measurements, the natural configurations of wood, and his imagination.

To make this child's willow chair, use seasoned wood of any kind for the frame of the chair, but use only green wood for the armrests, headrests, and spokes—the pieces that require bending.

MATERIALS

Branches for the Frame:

2 back leg posts (A) 1-1/2" diameter x 21"
2 front leg posts (B) 1-1/2" diameter x 21"
10 rails (2 C's, 2 D's, and 1 F, G, H, I, M, and N) 1" diameter x 16"
2 rails (E) 1" diameter x 18"
1 head support (J) 1-1/2" diameter x 18"
1 back arm support (K) 1-1/2" diameter x 18"
1 cross brace (L) 1" diameter x length needed (see instructions)

Armrests:

10 rods 1/2" diameter x 48"

Headrest:

5 rods 1/2" diameter x 96"

Spokes:

12 rods 1/2" diameter x 60"

Miscellaneous:

assortment of galvanized flathead nails: 2-1/2", 2", 1-1/2", 1", 3/4", and 1/2" wire brads

Note: After cutting the wood pieces for the frame, whittle around the cuts to smooth the edges. Use the rods to make the armrests, headrest, and spokes within a day of cutting, while they are still pliable (or stand the rods upright in a bucket of water to keep them supple for a few days).

TOOLS

saw
pruning shears
penknife
2 metal spring clamps
hammer

INSTRUCTIONS

Making the Frame

1. Working on a low, level surface, lay out one back leg post (A) and one front leg post (B). Incline the back post slightly, and position one of the 16" rails (C) in place horizontally 1" from the bottom of the leg posts. The rail should have a 1" overhang at each end. When you are satisfied with the placement, nail the pieces together.

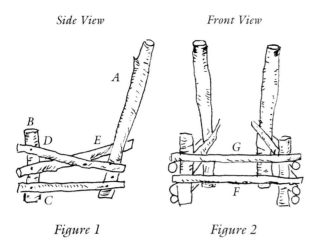

Side View   *Front View*

Figure 1   *Figure 2*

2. Position one rail (D) on an angle, as shown in Figure 1, so that it connects the front and back leg posts. Using one nail at each end, secure it in place. Attach one rail (E) in a diagonal from the back side of the back post to the front side of the front post and behind rail (D). (See Figure 1.)

3. Repeat steps 1 and 2 to make the other side of the chair frame in the same way.

4. Stand the sides of the chair upright with the two back posts slightly closer together than the front posts, as shown in Figure 2. Nail the horizontal rails (F) and (G) to the front of the front leg posts, again leaving a 1" overhang at each end.

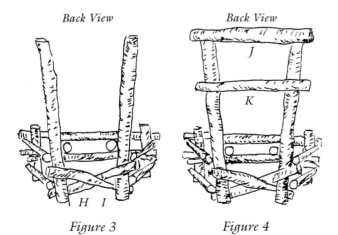

Back View   *Back View*

Figure 3   *Figure 4*

5. Turn the frame around, spread the tops of the back posts slightly, and nail two rails, (H) and (I), diagonally across the lower part of the back. As shown in Figure 3, each extends from the inside of one back post to the outside of the other back post.

6. Position the 18" head support piece (J) across the top ends of the back posts (see Figure 4), and nail it in place. Then nail the back arm support piece (K) to the back of the back posts halfway between the floor and the top. The back arm support (K) should extend approximately 2-1/2" on each side of the back posts.

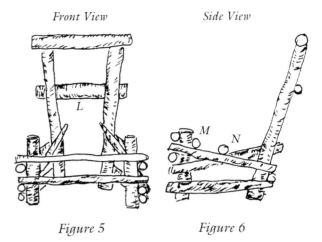

Front View   *Side View*

Figure 5   *Figure 6*

7. In line with the back arm support (K), measure the exact distance between the two back posts, and cut a piece of 1"-diameter wood to that length. Nail this piece (L) between the back posts in front of (K), as shown in Figure 5.

8. Position one rail (M) across the front of the chair and inside the front leg posts. As shown in Figure 6, it rests on top of the side rail (D). Nail (M) to the inside of the front leg post. Attach another rail (N) across the middle of the seat, and nail it to the intersections of rails (D) and (E). (Again see Figure 6.)

Adding Armrests

Note: You may find it helpful to refer to the photograph of the chair when attaching the armrests, headrest, and spokes.

9. Insert the base end of one 1/2"-diameter rod behind the bottom front rail (F) and inside the front post. (See Figure 7.) Nail the rod to (F) from the inside of the frame. Bend the rod in front of and above the leg post and clamp it to the end of the back arm support (K) at the outside of the back leg post. Repeat the same process with a second rod on the other side of the chair.

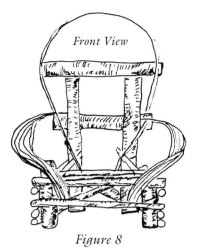

Figure 8

Building the Headrest

12. Position and clamp the base end of one 1/2"-diameter rod to the inside of the side diagonal rail (E). As illustrated in Figure 8, bring the rod around the ends of the back arm and head supports, bending it high above the head support. Clamp the rod inside the diagonal rail on the other side of the frame. Adjust the curve as desired, trim the end of the rod, and nail the rod to the side rails (E) and to the ends of the back arm and head supports. (See Figure 8.)

13. Add the other headrest rods, alternating base and tip ends on each side. Position each additional rod slightly forward from the last to give the finished headrest an inward-turning line. Nail the rods together as you did for the arms.

10. Due to the tension of the bent rods, the frame of the chair may become warped as you add the arm rods. Adjust the rods until the frame is square and the curves of the arm rods are similar and pleasing. Remove one clamp at a time, and nail the rods in place. Trim the end of each rod at least 1" from the nail to avoid splitting the wood.

11. Alternate sides and add all other armrest rods, working toward the inside at the front rail and toward the outside at the back arm support. Keep the rods close together and parallel, nailing them together successively with small brads placed every 5" or 6".

Front View

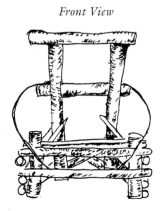

Figure 7

Installing the Seat/Back Spokes

14. Starting just left or right of the center front, butt the base end of one 1/2"-diameter rod against the inside of the front rail (G) and nail it to rails (M) and (N). Bend the rod firmly to make it dip at the back of the seat, curve it up against the back arm and headrest supports, and place it in position behind the headrest. Trim it flush with the top of the headrest. Attach the rod to the back arm and headrest supports by nailing through the rod into the headrest.

15. Alternately attach the remaining spokes to either side of the center, gently fanning and crossing them across the back of the chair.

16. To finish off your chair, cut a 1/2"-diameter rod 13" long, split it in half lengthwise with a penknife, and nail the half-round piece across the inside front of the seat to cover the cut ends of the spokes.

Twig Tea Table
see photo page 9

The desire to bring the tranquilizing influence of the forest into our lives dates back to the middle of the 18th century, when the first rustic garden tables appeared in Europe. Legend says that gypsies were the first to make willow furniture, gathering their willow in the spring "when the sap is up" and the branches are most pliable.

With just a dozen straight willow (or alder) branches you can make this delightful twig tea table in just a few hours. The classic design blends beautifully with casual indoor or outdoor patio furniture. The dimensions given here are suitable for a coffee table, but you can easily adjust the lengths to make a dining table or end table for your deck or patio.

MATERIALS

4 table top pieces, each 1-1/2" diameter
    x 22-1/2" long
4 diagonal pieces, each 1-1/2" diameter
    x 8" long
4 leg posts, each 1-1/2" diameter x
    18-1/2" long
1 piece of glass 21-1/2" square
(10) 2" and (24) 2-1/2" zinc-coated
    finishing nails

TOOLS

saw
hammer
T-square
measuring tape
electric drill
sanding disc or sand paper
knife

INSTRUCTIONS

1. After cutting the willow pieces, whittle around the cuts to smooth (and slightly round) the ends.

2. Working on a level surface, lay out the four table-top frame pieces. Before joining these four table-top frame pieces end to end, each table-top piece must be shaped to have one flat-cut (or notched) end and one rounded end.

Figure 1

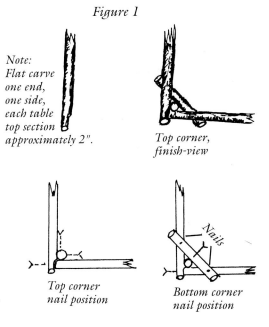

Note:
*Flat carve
one end,
one side,
each table
top section
approximately 2".*

*Top corner,
finish-view*

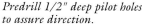

*Top corner
nail position*

*Bottom corner
nail position*

Nails

*Predrill 1/2" deep pilot holes
to assure direction.*

3. To make the flat-cut end, lightly whittle (or flatten down) about 2" on one side of one end of each frame piece. Cut the flattened "notch" so that it comfortably accommodates the rounded end of an adjoining frame piece. The rounded ends should fit snugly against the notch. (See Figure 1.)

4. Mark the matching ends to assure the best fit for the frame pieces.

5. Join the four wood pieces to create the square table-top frame. ALL nail holes should be pre-drilled to a depth of 3/4" to properly assure the correct angle. Nail through the notched side of one frame piece into the center of the rounded end of the adjoining piece. Continue around the top until all four sides are connected, forming a square frame to hold a glass top as level as possible.

Hint: It helps to set the pieces on a flat surface, and use a wall or other support to brace the end of the piece being nailed. Uneven knots can be sanded flat later.

6. Turn your assembled table-top frame upside down, and attach each leg piece into the inside angle of each corner with two nails (one nail into each top piece). Be sure to pre-drill all of the starting holes, and brace the pieces as you drive in the nails.

7. With the table frame still upside down and legs sticking up, attach one of the 8" diagonals across each inside corner. Use a T-square to assure a correct 90° joint at each corner; then drive one nail through each end of the diagonals into the under side of the table-top frame pieces. The diagonals must be placed tightly against the legs to help strengthen and support the legs.

Use the shorter, 2" finishing nails here to prevent the nails from coming through the table-top frame pieces. Be alert to this possibility. (Figure 2 shows the completed frame.)

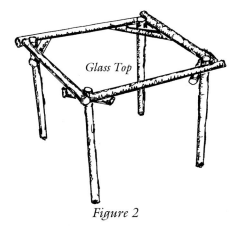

Glass Top

Figure 2

8. With one 2-1/2" coated finishing nail, nail through the 8" diagonal piece, into the adjoining leg piece (again be sure to brace the leg as you nail).

9. The number of nails suggested should be more than sufficient to maintain adequate strength; however, if you feel it is necessary to firm up certain joints, carefully pre-drill and add more nails. Remember that too many nails tend to weaken rather than strengthen your joint.

10. Sand all rounded ends, protruding knots, or noticeably uneven areas of the table-top frame pieces; this will assure a level fit for the glass top.

11. Measure the table-top frame to determine the exact dimensions for the glass top. The glass should reach from the center of one frame piece to the center of the opposite frame piece. A glass piece 21-1/2" square, of double thickness, should be ideal. Heavier glass is optional.

Hint: Slide a piece of paper under the glass to determine any high spots that need to be sanded for a better fit.

Wild Willow Branch Basket

see photo page 9

This delightful basket frame is built from 18" and 10" willow lengths, and it is constructed "upside down." All you need to make it are some willow saplings a little more than 1" in diameter. And no matter how limited your basketmaking skills, you can easily make this rectangular design in just an hour. Always an eye-catcher, this nifty little twig basket makes a conversation piece at the front door or on a deck or patio when it is filled with blooming potted plants nestled in a lining of Spanish moss.

MATERIALS

    willow saplings (alder, or other) about
        1-1/4" diameter
    1-3/4" coated finishing nails
    Spanish moss
    potted plants

TOOLS

    saw
    hammer
    ruler
    sandpaper
    drill with 1/16" bit

INSTRUCTIONS

Notes: Using sapling pieces that are consistent in diameter will result in a more attractive basket. All nailing is much easier if you pre-drill the holes 1/2" deep using a 1/16" bit.

1. First cut the willow saplings into 19 pieces, each 18" long, and 11 pieces, each 10" long. These measurements are from tip to tip. Sand the ends sparingly.

2. On a flat surface, lay two 18" wood pieces of equal diameter next to one another (parallel). Mark both pieces identically with seven equally spaced attachment points, about 2" apart.

3. Lay out seven of the 10" pieces, setting them on the marks made in step 2, above. Nail the

pieces in place onto the two 18" pieces. This is your basket base.

Optional: When you are beginning your base, you can add more 10" crosspieces to make a firmer, more solid bottom to the basket.

4. Begin making the two longer sides by placing two more 18" lengths on top of the first row of 10" cross pieces. Position them directly above the first two 18" pieces used for the base. Nail them in place.

5. Make the first row of the shorter sides by placing two of the 10" pieces across each end and nailing them in place.

6. Continue to build up the sides by placing two more of the 18" lengths on top of the ends of the two 10" pieces positioned in the previous step. Nail them in place.

7. Place two more of 10" pieces across each end, and secure them with nails.

8. Place the last two 18" pieces on top, and nail them into position. Your basket is now finished and ready for a lining of Spanish moss. Place one or more flower pots inside the moss-filled basket.

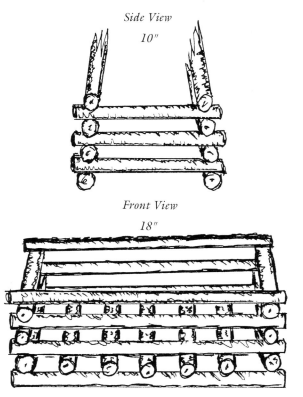

Side View

10"

Front View

18"

Willow Whip Birdcage

see photo page 15

Natural materials make a birdcage that is reminiscent of the outdoors. This one is made from willow whips and reed, which are suggestive of fields, woods, and quiet streams.

Willow shoots are easy to find in fields near water, and in ditches along country roads. Look for them in early spring, when the shoots are two to three feet tall. You can make this willow birdcage with just 36 willow shoots, twining the stems together with pieces of reed that shape the cage beautifully and hold it all together.

If you're a beginner at basketry, or if you just need a refresher, refer to the chapter called "Nature Craft Basics." This project assumes some familiarity with the basic techniques that are described there.

MATERIALS

36 willow shoots
an 8" hank of #2 reed
a few short strips of raffia
light-colored posterboard
moss
dried flowers and leaves
white spray paint (optional)

TOOLS

clippers
gloves
scissors
large kettle

INSTRUCTIONS

1. Strip the leaves from the willow shoots with gloved hands, moving from top to bottom. They should be long enough to make a cage that is approximately 24" tall.

2. Holding all of the shoots together, bend them in a circle and fit them into your cooking kettle. Fill the kettle with water almost to the top. Cover the kettle with a lid, and cook the shoots for 40 minutes.

3. Pour off the water; then let the willow shoots cool.

4. Peel the bark back from the bottom end and pull. The bark will slip off easily, showing the waxy white wood of the shoots.

5. Pick out 18 of the shoots and hold the ends together with rubber bands placed 5-6" from the ends of the stems.

6. With the #2 reed, begin weaving over and under. Make six rows woven closely together to hold the top firmly.

7. Now add one new willow whip to each of the 18 original willow pieces, slipping the new lengths alongside the existing ones. Place the top ends of the new pieces into the over, under weaving that already holds the first shoots together. There are now 36 willow whips in all.

8. Bend a new reed weaver in half, slip the center of the reed around one of the willow stems (stakes), and twine two rows (about 1" below the top), weaving over and under.

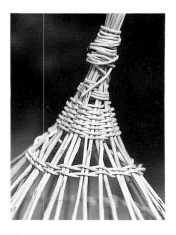

9. Next twine two more rows approximately 3" below the rows last twined.

Twining will automatically space the reeds quite evenly. Using the illustration (page 24) as a guide, shape the cage gently outward until you reach the approximate midpoint. For the area below the center of cage (the widest part), begin to twine the rows a little tighter and firmer. Shape the cage so that the bottom narrows.

10. Twine two more rows 3" below the last twined rows.

11. Now twine four rows approximately 2" below the two rows above.

12. Twine two more rows approximately 3" below the last four.

13. Using two reeds as one, twine two rows to shape a small base below what will be the door for the cage (see the illustration).

14. Twine ten rows (using a single reed), again shaping the stakes toward the base. When it is finished, the cage is approximately 24" tall.

Adding the Door and a Perch

15. Choose a place near the middle of the cage—between the four twined rows and two twined rows—for the door. (See the illustration.) Cut two of the stakes just under the edge of the four twined rows and just above the two twined rows to make an opening approximately 3" x 4".

16. Cut twelve 3" pieces of the #2 reed, and arrange the pieces in six groups of two. These will form the door.

17. With a single reed, weave over and under the twelve pieces. Begin to weave at the center (this holds the pieces more evenly), and weave from the center to the bottom. Then slip the reed back up to the center, going along the hinge side of the door. Now weave from the center to the top edge of the door.

18. End the weaving at the top by looping the door to a main stake on the cage, making a hinge for the door.

19. Take single strips of braided raffia to make a tie to fasten the door shut.

20. To make a perch, first measure the width across the center of the cage. Then cut eight pieces of reed to this measurement.

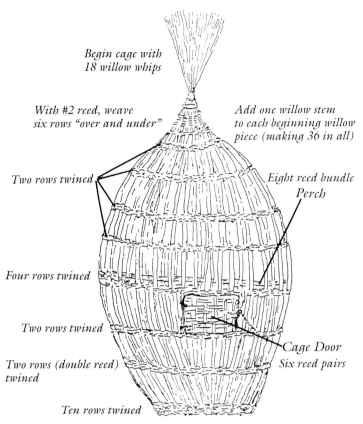

Begin cage with 18 willow whips

With #2 reed, weave six rows "over and under"

Add one willow stem to each beginning willow piece (making 36 in all)

Two rows twined

Eight reed bundle Perch

Four rows twined

Two rows twined

Cage Door
Six reed pairs

Two rows (double reed) twined

Ten rows twined

21. Wrap the bundle of eight reeds with a single reed 6" longer than the bundle. Use a spiral wrapping around the reed bundle, and leave a few extra inches of reed hanging at each end. After wrapping the reed around the full length of the bundle, bend the extra few inches of reed at each side down through the four twined rows. Secure the perch bundle in place by weaving the excess reed from side to side into the four twined rows.

Finishing

22. Measure the width of the cage just above the bottom rows.

23. Cut a circle out of a piece of light-colored posterboard, preferably light buff or white. Slip the board up inside the bottom opening of the cage to rest as flat as possible against the vertical reeds.

24. Lightly glue moss on the top surface of the removable posterboard piece. Cover it with dried flowers and leaves.

25. *Optional:* For the look of white wicker, spray paint the entire cage.

Be My (Honeysuckle) Valentine

see photo page 14

Year-round reminders of love, delicate wreaths made of honeysuckle vines come right from the heart of nature. Pull on your hiking boots, and head for the wild honeysuckle to gather these long, flexible vines.

MATERIALS

about 20 honeysuckle vines
flowers (dried or silk)
decorator ribbon with wire edge
12" square board
3" nails

TOOLS

scissors
large cooking pot
garden gloves
glue gun

INSTRUCTIONS

1. Coil the vines as you collect them so that they can fit in a pot at home. Boiling is needed to make them pliable and keep them from shrinking after they have been shaped.

2. Put the vines in a pot and boil them for two hours to loosen the bark (you can slide the bark off later with your gloved hand), or boil them for an hour to retain the bark, which gives you a darker, woodsy-looking vine.

3. Cool the vines a bit after boiling, and drain off the water. Vines boiled for two hours can be stripped of their outer skins easily. Run a gloved hand down these vines to remove the bark.

4. Let the vines dry in a coil, and you can store them until you want to use them. Soak the vines for five or ten minutes before you intend to use them.

5. Twist several vine lengths into a ropelike form; this will be handled like one long piece. Grasp the bundle of vines at the center using both hands. Then shape the bundle into a circle about 8" to 10" in diameter, letting the ends overlap.

6. Holding the top of the loop with one hand, pull one set of ends around from the back into the inside of the circle in a spiral motion. Wrap the vines around and around, and tuck the ends of each vine securely inside the wreath. Do the same with the other set of vine ends. The wreath will hold its shape without ties.

7. With thick vines, you'll only be able to spiral around about two times. If the vines are smaller and more flexible, your wraps can be much closer together, and you will see a definite spiral pattern.

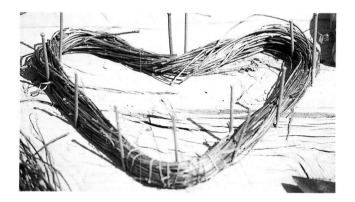

8. Using a 12" square board heavy enough to hold nails, draw a heart design that is approximately 8" to 10" across at its top width. Then draw a second, smaller heart within the first heart design.

9. Alternate 3" nails around the heart design, placing the first nail on the outer heart, and the next on the inside heart, as shown in the photograph. The nails should be hammered in only far enough to keep them firm in the wood.

10. Dampen the wreath and press it gently into the heart design.

Hold the wreath in the desired heart shape; the nails can be moved if necessary to help hold the wreath tightly. Hammer the nails more firmly into the board, and allow the vines to dry completely in the heart form.

11. Lift the vine heart wreath away from the nails when it has dried completely.

12. Follow your own taste in decorating your wreath. Florists' greenery and baby's breath, silk flowers, and ribbons of satin and lace are all appropriate for a naturalistic valentine.

Downy Woodpecker Door Knocker

see photos page 12

Knock, knock. Who's there? Your first introduction to woodpeckers will probably come when you hear one tapping away as it splits the bark of a tree. Without even seeing this bird you can tell from the sound of its drumming which species of woodpecker inhabits your woods.

Did you know that each species has its own special hammering note? For example, the large pileated woodpecker hammers an average of 12 strokes increasing in force and frequency toward the middle of the sequence and fading off toward the end. The short rat-a-tat of the robin-sized hairy woodpecker has loud and deliberate, well-spaced taps. The closely related downy woodpecker gives a softer, longer, and more rapid drumming sequence.

Here the downy, our most familiar woodpecker, becomes a delightful door knocker in a folk-art design from the early 1900s. He is made of solid wood and hand painted in the same colors as the original. A more natural paint design also is included as an alternative. With a lacquer finish, he is durable outdoors, as a most efficient and entertaining door knocker for everyone, kids and adults alike.

The bird is cut from 1 x 6 pine, preferably a piece without knots and with an even grain for easier cutting. The bird is mounted onto a small, split log about 10" long, and a leather cord attached to the foot of the bird activates the knocking of the woodpecker's beak on the log.

MATERIALS

    1 piece of 1 x 6 pine, 10" long
    1 log or branch, 10" long
    12" leather shoelace
    1 wooden bead
    3" finishing nail
    screw eye
    sandpaper
    tracing paper
    red, black, and white acrylic paints
    varnish or lacquer

TOOLS

    small hand axe
    electric saber saw or hand-held coping saw
    drill
    small chisel
    #2 and #6, or #8 and #10 paint brushes
    1" varnish brush

INSTRUCTIONS

1. Enlarge the bird pattern, and trace it onto your piece of wood. Then, using an electric saber saw or a hand-held coping saw, cut along the lines of the pattern, taking special care not to split the wood at the beak.

2. Sand all of the edges until they are smooth to the touch.

3. Split a 10" log or tree branch with a hand axe to a thickness of 3/4". If you have never before split a log, use the following procedure:
    A. Select a log without knots; it is easier to split.
    B. Scratch an imaginary line across the center of one end of the log.
    C. Set the log on end on a solid surface.
    D. Drive a hand axe, or a metal wedge hammer, into the split line (a good Boy Scout hatchet will do the job if the proper tools are not available).
    E. The log should split evenly. Choose the best half for your project.

4. Measure 4" from the top of the split log, and drill a 1/4" hole through the wood; then drill a second hole 7" down from the top of the log.

5. Chisel out the wood between the two holes to accommodate the bird's "foot" projection.

6. Starting at the second hole, use a narrow wood chisel to gouge a channel 1/2" deep in the back (flat side) of the log. (If you don't have a chisel, try using a screw driver.) The channel should run all the way from the second hole to the bottom end of the log. The leather pull-cord will hang down through this channel.

7. Now drill a small hole crosswise, halfway down the slot that will hold the bird's foot projection.

8. This small hole should accommodate a 3" finishing nail that will form an axis on which the bird rocks back and forth. The nail also slips through a matching hole drilled in the bird's foot projection (note the location of the hole in the illustration).

Pattern for Cutting and Painting

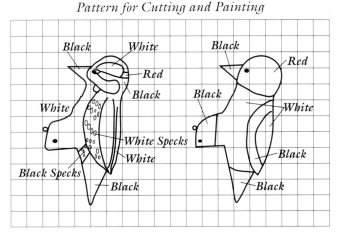

To Scale: 1 square = 3/4"

9. As shown in the illustration above, insert a small screw eye in the edge of the foot projection. Then tie the leather shoelace to the small screw eye.

10. To paint the bird pattern, use:
Nos. 2 and 6 brushes (for hairy woodpecker)
Nos. 8 and 10 brushes (for downy woodpecker)
1"-wide varnish brush
Acrylic paints: red/black/white
Varnish or lacquer for the final coat

11. Mount your painted woodpecker on the log by first placing the foot projection through the slot. Then slip the finishing nail into the holes drilled for it in the log and in the bird's foot projection.

12. Tie a wooden bead onto the end of the leather shoelace so that the pull-cord will hang down about 6" below the bottom end of the log. Adjust the length of the pull-cord to create the proper weight to balance the knocker and return the bird to the correct position after each knock.

13. Mount the door knocker using a nail or a single screw placed at the top of the split log.

A Cattail Basket
Weave with Leaves
see photo page 16

Weave cattail leaves and willow whips to make this attractive Indian basket. Cut the green cattail leaves at the height of their growth, anytime between May and December. Use whip—freshly cut if possible—from the new sprouts of "creek willow" growing near water. Sprouts emerging from a clear-cut area or the new shoots of pussy willow also make good spokes for your basket.

Lay the cattail leaves flat to dry; that prevents shrinkage after the basket is done. Re-dampen them for ease in weaving over the willow-whip spokes.

Choose the least tapered willow spokes to cut. Then, by running your hand from the tip to the base, strip away the leaves, and the whips are ready for weaving. Willow whips that have dried thoroughly never completely regain their fresh-cut pliability, even when soaked in water. It is possible to keep the whips pliable for several days after cutting them by wrapping them in wet paper, leaves, or cloth, or by standing them in a tall bucket of water.

MATERIALS

cattail leaves
willow whips
raffia

TOOLS

knife or scissors to cut cattails and willow
large-eyed needle

INSTRUCTIONS

1. Begin making this basket, which will be about 8" across and 7" high, by cutting six pieces of willow, each 22" long.

2. Cross the six whips in two groups of three (as shown in Figure 1).

3. Tuck the end of a soaked cattail leaf inside and under a spoke, and hold it there as you begin to wrap the leaf around the crossed groups of spokes. You're anchoring them for further

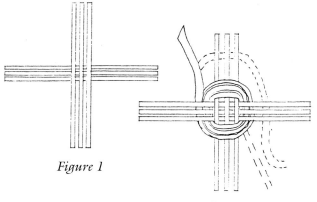

Figure 1

Figure 2

weaving. Wrap over and under the groups of spokes three times (as in Figure 2).

4. Now, before you begin the actual weaving, add one more spoke to make the total an uneven number. Cut a piece of willow 11" long. Tucking it into the cattail wrapping, notice that you now have 13 spokes (see "A" in Figure 2).

5. Continue with your cattail leaf, now weaving over and under the individual willow spokes (see Figure 3).

6. Gently spread the spokes apart as you weave, coaxing them into an evenly spaced pattern similar to spokes radiating from the hub of a wheel. As you weave outward from the center, the spokes become farther apart. Slip in another two spokes (each 11" long), poking each new spoke into the weaving (Figure 3).

7. Continue to weave, securing the added spokes. Later, add another pair of 11" spokes so that you are now weaving over and under 17 in total.

8. When you reach the end of a cattail leaf, overlap it with a new one, and weave the two as one for a couple of strokes to secure the ends. Then continue weaving with the new leaf.

9. As your weaving reaches about 5" in diameter, give the whole thing a good soaking. If you're near a stream, hold it in the water. The pieces may break if they are allowed to dry too much.

10. Then begin to bend the willow spokes upward to form a bowl shape. Holding the basket against your body makes it easier to shape it while you are weaving.

Decide how high you want the sides to be, perhaps just tall enough to hide a flower pot. You'll need to leave 3" to 4" of spoke to finish the basket with a scalloped edge.

For a Scalloped Edge
11. Soak the basket well before trying to bend the spokes into this border design. Then bend one spoke, bringing it around the outside of the nearest spoke, and poking it down alongside the spoke that is next closest. The end should be inserted about 2" into the weaving. Repeat with each spoke in turn. The willow whips make a strong rim when they are bent over and down like this.

For a Soft Rim
12. This is another pretty border; you can see it on the finished basket photographed. Start by cutting off the spokes just above the weaving. Thread a needle with raffia, strong grass, or a narrow braid of cattail leaves. Bundle together four cattail leaves. Holding the bundle atop the raw edge, whipstitch the bundle to the basket rim. Stitch all the way around in one direction; then stitch in the reverse direction to make a very firm, finished border.

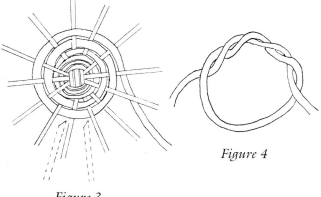

Figure 4

Figure 3

Securing the Basket Base
13. A willow circle stitched to the bottom holds the basket upright, and discourages wobbling or tipping. Grasping a long willow whip at the center, cross the ends to make a circle about 3" in diameter. Then, holding the loop in one hand, wrap the ends around the loop to make a twist (as shown in Figure 4). With your needle threaded with raffia, sew the twisted circle of willow to the bottom of the basket. Position the circle so that the basket stands straight and upright.

From Wool to
Felt Purse and Slippers

see photo page 11

Spring to the farmer has always meant the time for shearing the sheep. Thick, wonderful wool is then made into fabric and yarn. Felting the wool provides us with a quick and simple way to make woolen fabric; no special skills or equipment are required.

An ancient textile, felt is still made today much as it was long ago. A legend about the discovery of felt says that Noah, in an effort to make his ark more comfortable, padded the floor with sheep's wool. By the time 40 days and nights had passed, the loose wool had turned into a matted fabric—felt—from the pressure and moisture of the animals.

Felt caps as old as 3,500 years have been found in Scandinavia, and others dating from the Bronze Age (1400–1200 B.C.) were found in Germany and Siberia. Mongolians lived in felt houses, wore felt boots, and carried felt bags and purses.

Most animal-hair fibers will form some kind of felt, but the fibers closest to sheep's wool work best. Mohair (from the Angora goat), with its relatively long, coarse fibers, will tend to felt like a long-staple wool. Llama wool is probably similar.

Handmade felt slippers and felt clutch purses have a special, warm texture that you want to touch—and they can be made in one day! You can find white, natural, or colored wool in most spinning and weaving shops.

MATERIALS

Wool in rolags: approximately 4 oz. cleaned and carded for one pair of small slippers or one small purse
nylon netting, 48" long x 24" wide
dental floss or heavy thread
detergent

TOOLS

long needle
tea kettle
rubber gloves
rolling pin

pencil
paper
scissors
yarn needle and yarn, or sewing machine

INSTRUCTIONS

Making the Felt

1. Cut two pieces of the nylon netting, each approximately 24" x 24" (big enough to cover the layers of wool batting).

2. Begin layering the rolags (the rolls of carded wool) on one piece of the nylon netting. Lay the rolags next to one another, overlapping them slightly at the edges. Next, lay the second layer of rolag pieces perpendicular to the first, and the third layer perpendicular to the second. Spread the wool as evenly as you can throughout the batt (the layers of rolags). You must use at least two layers for the slippers; three layers make a better thickness for a purse.

Note: The proper placement of these rolags is the most important step; it is the foundation for the felt. The wool rolag pieces must overlap each other to make a strong piece of felt. Areas that are too thin will leave holes. The strongest felts in the felt industry today are those made by hand with rolags laid perpendicularly.

3. Cover the batt with the other piece of nylon netting, and pin the two nylon pieces together, ready to baste.

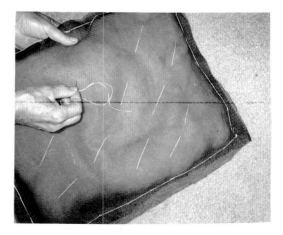

4. Using the dental floss or heavy thread, sew long, loose stitches around the edges of the entire batt. Next make long quilting stitches on the diagonal across the batt in rows about 3" apart.

5. Place the batt in the kitchen sink, or in a tub, and saturate it with boiling water. The moisture and heat cause the fibers to swell and the scales of the wool begin to open.

6. Using detergent (soap or liquid) and more hot water, and wearing your rubber gloves, rub the soap into the batt. Work the batt with your hands (you can remove your gloves as the water cools), kneading it from side to side. This process is called hardening.

7. With a rolling pin or similar tool, roll over the batt in all directions and on both sides. Roll it and unroll it as you do the hardening.

The batt can be put in the bathtub, where hot water, soap and stamping it with feet can do the hardening very effectively. A wet batt is somewhat delicate; don't handle it too roughly, or it might tear apart.

8. When you think the felt is hardened (pull on it gently to see if the wool is firm and will not pull apart), cut the threads and take off the nylon netting. Continue to do the "fulling" (hardening) a bit longer with the batt now uncovered.

If you see any holes in the batt, this is the time for you to fill them in with more wool. Put some of the carded wool in and around the hole, cover it with hot water and soap, and work it gently. Work the filled area harder; then work the whole batt again. You can actually change the shape of the batt at this time, while the felt is soft (i.e., the edges can be cut into forms, folded, or made thicker).

9. Rinse the batt well, roll it up in one or two towels; then press out the moisture, and let the batt dry.

Sewing a Purse

10. Make a pattern for a small purse in the shape that you like. Lay out the pattern onto the dry felt, pin it in place, and cut.

11. Using a sewing machine (on a long stitch setting), or a needle and thread, stitch the larger pieces together. The smaller felt pieces can be glued into place. You can also glue or stitch decorative cording along the edges or add other enhancements.

Felt Slippers

12. First make sure that you have patterns that are the correct size. Using Figure 1 as a reference, make a pattern for the left sole 1" larger than the foot all around. Repeat with the other foot, and cut out the patterns along the outlines.

13. On another sheet of paper, draw and cut out the patterns for the sides of the slippers. (You need two top pieces for each slipper.)

14. Pin or glue the top pieces together along the seam edges, and glue or pin the top to the sole along the seams. Try the paper slipper for size, and adjust your patterns if necessary.

15. Place all of the paper patterns (two soles and four side pieces in all) onto your felt, pin them in place, and cut.

16. Pin the side pieces together at the front and back, with right sides facing out. Then stitch (by machine or by hand) through the two layers. If you stitch by hand, use wool yarn (or heavier, button hole thread) and a crewel needle, and make a blanket stitch. (See Figure 2.)

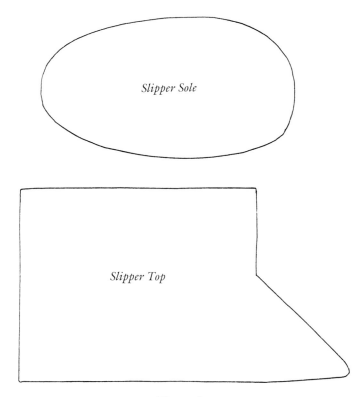

Slipper Sole

Slipper Top

Figure 1

Figure 2

17. Stitch the back heel edges together from top to bottom. Stitch the front open edges together starting about 1" down from the top edge. Fit the slipper top onto the sole, pinning the open edges all around the slipper.

18. Using wool yarn (or button hole thread) and a crewel needle, stitch around the open edges of the entire slipper (from the sole to the slipper top). Make a blanket stitch with the stitches approximately 1/4" apart.

19. You can apply decorations made of felt or leather to customize your slippers. If you expect heavy wear, stitch lightweight leather soles onto the felt soles.

Nature's Easter Egg Dye

see photo page 10

In the 18th century, it was common for people to dye eggs for Easter using the juice from wild berries, cooked bark, and vegetables such as red cabbage and onions. The early pioneers of Kansas also used onion skins, walnut hulls, bark, and other natural material for dyeing. Easter eggs were wrapped in onion skins and placed in a hot salt or vinegar bath to make them red or yellow. The stain of ripe berries was used to create dull blues and purples.

Naturally dyed eggs have very interesting and sometimes unexpected colors. Red cabbage, for instance, turns eggshells a bluish purple color. If you cook the eggs in onion skins, they turn a pretty red and yellow; berry juices dye the eggs pale pink or blue.

MATERIALS

white eggs for dyeing
yellow onion skins (for a yellow-orange color)
red onion skins (pale blue)
fresh red cabbage (medium to deep blue)
paprika (light pink to orange)
walnut shells (deep rich brown)
dried sassafras root (medium to deep orange)
fresh or frozen blueberries (pale purple or
   blue)
vinegar
raw egg white (optional)
dried flowers, etc. for decorations (optional)

Note: Try other fresh roots, berries, barks, and flowers that are available where you live.

TOOLS

knife
measuring spoons
saucepans (one for each color)
small bowls (one for each color)

INSTRUCTIONS

1. Chop or shred the vegetable pieces, shells, or roots before using them. You will need approximately one cup to make each batch of dye.

Approximately two tablespoons is a sufficient quantity for dried spices, roots, or berries.

2. Place the vegetable pieces or berries (use only one kind at a time) in a pot with three to four cups of water, and let them simmer for at least 30 minutes or until you see the color you like. Pour the dyed water into cups or smaller bowls, and add one teaspoon of vinegar per cup of dye.

Some eggs have an oily coating to retard spoilage. Before dyeing, you can clean the shell with a mix of vinegar and water. Eggs that are already hard boiled turn paler colors than do raw eggs. To get deep, rich colors, cook the eggs together with the vegetables about 20 minutes.

3. Slip the clean, white eggs into the natural dye, completely covering the eggs. Turn the eggs over and over while they are dyeing to make sure they are colored evenly. Don't let the eggs rest on the bottom or against the side of the pan.

4. Remove the eggs when they are as dark or light as you want, and lay them on paper towels to dry. Move them again in a minute so that the color doesn't begin spotting. Handle the eggs carefully after dyeing; some colors are only weakly absorbed by the eggshell and will scratch or chip easily.

5. You can dye designs onto your Easter eggs, and you can combine two or more colors. After the first dyeing, just tape designs, even names, onto the eggs using masking tape. Place the egg back in the same dye, or use another color, and leave it immersed until it becomes the color you want. Take the egg out of the dye, let it dry, then remove the tape. Your design will appear in a lighter (or contrasting) color.

6. Decorate the colored surface with pressed flowers, herbs, and small leaves. (Be sure to wait until the eggs are dry.) Use tweezers to hold the dry flower and leaf pieces while you lightly coat the underside of each flower or leaf with an adhesive.

If you plan to eat your colored eggs, do not use glue to attach any decorations. Raw egg white acts as a harmless, gentle adhesive to hold the decorations in place until you are ready to eat the eggs. Create your own delicate designs using tiny flowers and leaves on the soft colors of the naturally dyed eggs.

Nature's Easter Basket
With Willow Whips and Wisteria Vine
see photo page 10

Creating Easter baskets to fill with colored eggs and candies reminds us of nature's reawakening in springtime. This graceful basket is made with slender shoots of wisteria and willow whips, and it is decorated with bits of moss and dried flower blossoms.

A spring day's walk through the woods to gather vines is a delightful discovery process. On tree branches overhead, and hidden beneath leaves under foot, you'll see evidence of new growth. When searching for vines to make a basket, look for long runners, 36" or longer, of wisteria, honeysuckle, or other vines of a similar diameter. To make them easier to carry, coil the vines as you pull and cut them.

MATERIALS

8 willow whip pieces, each 24" long
several lengths of wisteria or honeysuckle vine
4 willow whip pieces, each 18" long
2 pieces of raffia or cord
Spanish moss
dried flower blossoms

TOOLS

scissors or clippers
awl or knitting needle
glue gun

INSTRUCTIONS

Note: For some helpful tips on weaving baskets, consult the chapter called "Nature Craft Basics."

1. Starting with the newly collected vines, rub off the leaves by pulling the vines through your gloved hand. Coil the stripped vines, and push them into a cooking pot (an enamelled soup kettle is ideal). Then cover the vines with water, and steam-boil them for about an hour. Boiling will keep the vines from shrinking after they are woven into baskets.

After one hour of boiling, turn off the heat and let everything cool. Then pour out the water and remove the coil of vines. You can use them immediately or hang them up to dry for weaving later.

If you want a white, waxy look for some of the vines in the design, rub off the bark by pulling the still-wet vines through your gloved hand. If you want to use the vines after they have dried thoroughly, soak them for five or ten minutes before starting to weave.

2. Begin with eight willow whip stakes, each 24" long. Make four pairs, overlap the pairs in their centers, and arrange them like the spokes in a wheel. (See the illustration.) This arrangement produces eight paired spokes.

3. Gently bend one wisteria or honeysuckle weaver in half, and slip the loop (the "bend" in the vine) around the bottom-most pair of stakes that are crossed. With this beginning loop of your weaver in place over the first pair of spokes (stakes) you are ready to begin the twining that you will do for the entire basket. It is a simple pattern that involves taking your weaver under and over as you work around the basket.

4. Refer to the illustration for guidance when beginning to twine. Moving clockwise, start at the loop, and take the part of the weaver that is under the first pair of spokes and bring it up over the second pair. Take the other half of the weaver (the part that is on top of the first pair of spokes), and twine it down under the second pair. The objective is to use the weavers to create loops around each pair of spokes as you twine. Continue around clockwise, twining over and under the spokes.

5. Hold the basket in one hand, shaping it gently as you go along, and press the weave close together so that you will have a good, tight basket. Weave around the eight pairs of willow stakes, twining, for four rounds.

6. Break down each pair of stakes to single willow whips (making a total of 16 stakes). Now twine around the 16 stakes until the base of the basket has a diameter of about 6". Then begin to upsett (the point at which you bend the stakes upward to start the sides). Gently pinch and bend the stakes while weaving firmly, (fixing the upsett).

Note: When you have used all of one vine weaver, simply end it behind a stake and lay your new weaver over it to continue.

You can make your basket as large as you want. This basket is about 4-1/2" high and reaches about 8" across from edge to edge. Of course no two baskets are exactly alike, and this is part of the fun!

7. With your willow stakes extending above the top edge of the basket approximately 4" or more, begin to make the scalloped border. Bend each willow end over to the next channel (stake opening). Use an awl or a knitting needle to ease the willow end firmly down into place. As you continue around the rim, make the border scallops all about the same size.

8. For the handle, cut four slim willow pieces about 18" long, and twist the pieces together for the basket handle. Tie the ends together with some dark cord or raffia. Make an opening alongside two opposing stakes, and insert the handle ends until they are firmly secured. For added security, tie the handle ends at the base and edge of the basket.

9. Add Spanish moss to the inside, bottom, and sides of the basket. Glue the moss into place with a glue gun. Dried flowers glued onto the handle or on the moss make an appealing Easter basket design.

A Child's Easter Basket

see photo page 15

Keepsake Easter baskets for the kids can be crafted entirely by hand with just a coil of willow reed. You need no special equipment; even as a beginner you can make these little baskets with relative ease. In just one evening, you can create not only a basket to please your aesthetic senses, but a useful work of art as well.

MATERIALS

1 coil of #4 round reed
raffia

TOOLS

awl or knitting needle
scissors or clippers
ruler
sink
towel

INSTRUCTIONS

Note: For some tips on weaving baskets, refer to the chapter on "Nature Craft Basics."

1. Cut 16 reed stakes, each 25" long (for either basket). Soak them in water for 10–20 minutes.

2. Pull six reed weavers at a time from the coil and soak them in the water.

3. Take the 16 stakes from the water, divide them into groups of four, and cross them over and under each other as shown in Figure 1.

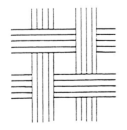

Figure 1

Cross stakes in
groups of four.

Figure 2

Lay weaver end over one
group of four stakes.

4. Begin the center by laying one end of the weaver over a group of four stakes (see Figure 2). Weave over and under the groups of four, making three identical rows around the stakes.

5. Pinch the weaver, and reverse the process (weave under where you had woven over) to coil in the opposite direction. Weave over and under three times around.

6. Cut one 6" reed to use as a bye-stake. Slip it in place between the center coils (between two of the groups of the four stakes).

7. Break down each group of four to two stakes, and continue weaving over and under the double stakes. Weave two rounds to make the saucer-shaped basket. The stakes will begin to bend upward. Continue weaving 16 more rows, gently shaping the basket as you weave.

To make the bowl-shaped baskets, weave three rounds. Then continue weaving the sides: 12 rows for the smaller basket, and 14 rows for the larger bowl-shaped basket. Soak the reed and the baskets periodically to keep them flexible.

8. To make a looped rim for the top of the basket, measure 4" on each stake from the last row of weaving, and trim off the excess. Soak the stakes for a few minutes before bending.

9. Each loop is formed by bending a stake and pushing its end down alongside the adjacent stake. Use a knitting needle or an awl to make a path for each stake before you bend it. Push the ends down the same distance each time so that the border loops are all approximately the same size (see Figure 3). The loops hold the basket together.

10. To make the handle shown on the saucer-shaped baskets, start with four 30" pieces of reed. After they have been soaked in water for a few minutes, grasp the pieces together in a bundle. Push the bundle up through one bottom opening, over two groups of four stakes, and down into the other opening as shown in Figure 4. Pull the reeds through until the handle is centered.

11. Break down the reeds from four to two, and lace two pairs of reeds up through adjacent loops on each side of the basket. (Refer to the photograph.)

12. Bring the ends together at the top, and wrap them together with tape. Finish the handle with a smooth wrapping of raffia. Tie a raffia or ribbon bow at the center of the handle.

13. To make the handle shown on the bowl-shaped basket, cut four 16" pieces of reed. After soaking them in water, divide the reed into two groups of two. Slide the pairs across the basket, using the awl or knitting needle to make a path through the weaving. Bring the ends together, and wrap them with raffia or ribbon.

14. Rub the baskets with vegetable oil to give them the look of varnished wicker.

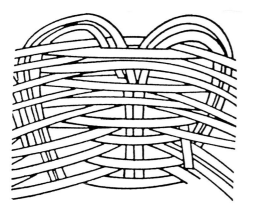

Figure 3

Push stake ends down alongside next stake.

Figure 4

Secure handle group of four stakes at bottom center, going up one opening and down through another.

Backyard Clay Vases

see photo page 16

Clay modeling is one of the world's oldest crafts. Nearly all peoples have made dishes or ornamental pieces from native clay. As early as 3000 B.C., Egyptians made glazed pottery, and the Chinese began making clay vessels thousands of years ago.

Without any previous experience, you can easily model by hand all of these pieces from moist clay and decorate them with delicate tones of acrylic paint. After applying a lacquer finish, you will have an exciting expression of your individual creativity made from unbaked clay.

MATERIALS

> 1 pound of clay
> acrylic paints, small pots in assorted colors
> small bottle of gesso (fast-drying acrylic primer)

TOOLS

> paint brushes (synthetic): flat #2 and #8, and liner #2
> optional items: cuticle scissors, small kitchen knife, craft knife, rolling pin, vaseline, cutting pliers

INSTRUCTIONS

Clay from Your Back Yard

If you don't already have clay on hand, you can dig some from your own backyard. The best time to dig clay is after a good rain. If you do dig into dry clay, wet it well before you begin working with it. Remove any hard stones or tiny pieces of wood that you find. Wet it, put it in a plastic bag, and pull out handfuls as you need pieces to shape for molding.

Clay should mold easily, like cookie dough. If it sticks to your hands, it is too wet. If it's too dry, sprinkle some water on the clay and knead it.

Long-Necked Vases

1. Pinch off a lump of clay about the size of a Ping-Pong ball. Roll the clay between the palms of your hands until it is quite round. Make a depression in the center of the ball of clay with your thumb or forefinger; the neck of the vase will slide into this depressed opening.

2. To make the stem (neck) of the vase, roll out a long piece of clay. Flatten it with a rolling pin or bottle to make the piece about 3" long by 1/2" wide. With a small cutting knife, cut the edges off straight and square. Next lay a pencil on one long edge of the clay, and roll the clay around the pencil. The clay should just cover the pencil with no overlap; cut and remove any excess clay. Before pinching the edges together around the pencil, open the clay out flat, and smear a little bit of vaseline onto the inner side of the clay that is facing the pencil (this allows easy removal of the pencil later). Re-wrap the clay around the pencil, and when you gently pinch the edges together, smooth the seam with your finger.

3. With the pencil still inside the roll of clay, insert this neck piece into the depressed center of the round base from step 1. Taper the clay between the two pieces by smoothing the clay gently where the neck and base meet. The vase quickly acquires a one-piece look.

4. Slide the pencil from inside the neck, and leave the vase to dry thoroughly before you begin to paint.

5. To achieve the appearance of a pitcher, just taper the sides with a small knife. Then roll out a piece about the diameter of your pencil, and attach it for a handle. Gently pinch the top edge of the vase slightly outward, making a small lip.

Wide-Mouthed Vases

6. Start by rolling the clay between the palms of your hands, making 12" x 1/2" (diameter) snakes. Coil one snake to start the center bottom of the vase, and build up the sides by coiling more rows. You can change the shape of the vase by changing the position of your coils. Smooth the sides with your fingers to eliminate the coil pattern, and smoothly pinch the edges of the top lip. If desired, roll out smaller clay rods to attach as handles.

7. Brush the vase with slip (a mix of water and clay that has the consistency of paint) to achieve a smooth clay surface on the outside, inside, lip, and at the attachment points for the handles. Let the vase dry thoroughly.

Painting the Clay Vases

8. After all of your clay pieces are completely dry, brush on one coat of gesso quickly and easily. Gesso is a fast-drying primer for the acrylic paints.

9. You can paint your vases a solid color or decorate them with painted designs. Fine lines are painted with a liner brush held perpendicular to the surface (thin the paint with a little water so that it flows freely through the brush hairs).

Acrylic paints are easy to work with because they are water soluble, easily blended, and dry fairly quickly. Have some water handy for thinning and blending. For example, you will get the prettiest blends of blue by experimenting. Add a little red for a pale purple shade, a little black for the more inky blue shade, white for a lighter grayish blue—or just wet the dab of blue directly from the paint pot and begin to paint.

10. Practice a few strokes on tracing paper; then continue until you have begun to fill the vase. To make designs similar to those done by many of the artisans in Portugal, include a squiggle, a scroll, a castle, a dog, a flower, and some of your own designs to create your own personal touch.

"For the Birds"
A Birdhouse of Vines

see photo page 13

Birds quickly take to this rustic birdhouse that looks much like their own work. Curly tendrils and irregular knots that occur randomly along the honeysuckle stems give the house a natural beauty. It is practical as well, for the roof can be removed to allow you to clean house between residents.

You can easily recognize honeysuckle, which abounds with white and yellow flowers and showy stamens during the summer. Usually found apart from cultivated gardens, it grows wild in the woods, shading native plants. Gathering the long, slim runners of honeysuckle vine is actually half the fun of making this birdhouse. If you don't have honeysuckle growing nearby, thin, flexible shoots of grape vine or wisteria vine will work just as well.

Birds do have a few preferences, and before making your honeysuckle birdhouse, you should consider which birds you want to occupy it. You want the house wide enough to accommodate their tail feathers and deep enough to suit their fancy. The size of the opening is also quite important. Some birds such as wrens, chickadees, purple martins, bluebirds, and great crested flycatchers prefer a hole just large enough for them to enter. Others—robins, barn swallows, and song sparrows—will only use shelters that are open on one or more sides. (The appendix on page 127 lists the preferences of several common birds.) Face the hole toward the south, and tip the house slightly to prevent rain from entering the hole.

MATERIALS

10–15 honeysuckle (or other thin, flexible) vines

TOOLS

scissors or knife

INSTRUCTIONS

1. After you have collected your vines, pull each one through a gloved hand (from tip to base), gently stripping off the tiny leaves.

2. Cut 16 spokes about 20" long, plus one pair 10" long. See the photograph of the base.

3. Take four groups of spokes, each having four vines, and cross them at their centers (see Figure 1).

4. Now insert the two half-length spokes (these are the shaded spokes marked "5" in Figure 1) in the middle of group "2." This addition gives an uneven number of spokes so that only one weaver is necessary.

5. Next, insert your first weaver under the group of four marked "1," carry it up under a diagonal group, and weave under and over the groups for three rounds.

6. Separate the spokes into pairs, and weave under and over, following the curved arrows. Each time around, the weaver will come out at an alternate pair.

7. Continue weaving in this manner to build up the sides of the birdhouse as shown in Figure 2. The distance from "A" to "B" is 3-1/2"; the diameter at "B" is 6"; the distance from "B" to "C" is about 2".

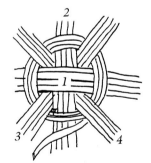

Figure 1

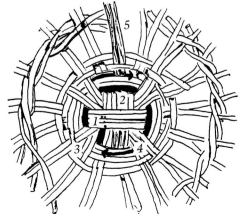

12. Finish the birdhouse by separating the spokes and using a closed border over the single spokes (see Figure 3).

Figure 3

13. Tie the roof onto the sides of the birdhouse at three places, as at "K."

14. Construct a perch by making a firm loop of twisted vines about 3" across, and secure the ends about 2" below the opening.

15. Referring to Figure 2, construct a hanger by looping a double strand of vine, and attaching it to the base of the rooftop. Bend the two ends upward, twist them once around in a circle, and interlock them through their own strands at the base of the loop. Now twist the ends a second time around in a circle, this time going at right angles to the first twist. Each twist locks around the strands beneath (see the shaded strands). Interlock the strands into the weaving at the top of the birdhouse roof. (Alternatively, a braid can be treated the same way.)

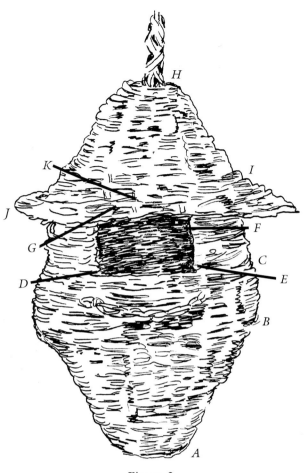

Figure 2

8. To make the opening, cut out two pairs of spokes. Conceal these ends in your weaving ("D" and "E" in Figure 2).

9. Weave back and forth at each side of the opening, "F," taking extra turns around the edges to fill in any gaps. Weave 1" above the opening to "G," and narrow the diameter to about 4". Now at "G," finish with a closed border (see Figure 3).

The Roof and Other Details

10. Weave your roof separately to extend over the sides of the house. Start the center just as you did the base, with 16 spokes, each 15" long, and later inserting the 17th pair.

11. As shown in Figure 2, you will weave a tent shape having a distance from "H" to "I" of 2-1/2". The diameter at "I" will be about 4-1/2" to match that at "G." Weave 2" farther to "J," where your diameter will be approximately 7" or 8".

The long, sultry days of summer invite a lazy stroll along the beach to search out colorful seashells and bits of driftwood.

Fat twigs in the full growth of summer make wonderful sketching pencils that easily fit the slight curve of your hand. Instructions can be found on page 68.

Ideal for beach combing, shopping, or just knocking around, these raffia sandals are guaranteed to fit when you make them yourself. They're stylish yet comfortable, and they can be embellished with beads, tropical flowers, or whatever suits your fancy. See page 50 for instructions.

A natural "window" made with rice paper and bamboo displays a scene composed of dried flowers and delicate leaves. Oriental in spirit and classic in design, it adds a natural warmth to any room. Directions are on page 49.

Hours spent on or near the water—whether it be ocean, lake, or mountain stream—hold a special significance for most of us. By making a permanent print of the fish that nearly got away, you can capture the drama and the energy of the moment you landed it. With wind chimes made from a handful of seashells, each gentle breeze brings a reminder of the shore. Instructions for the fish print are on page 58, and the wind chime can be found on page 57.

Summer is the perfect time to relax under a shade tree with a good book. And there is no more appropriate way to mark your page than with a bookmark made with pressed flowers. See page 53 for directions.

Because of their wide variety of shape, size, and color, sedum plants make a splendid, live-action wreath that changes almost daily as the plants mature. An altogether different look can be achieved with familiar ivy cuttings. Tucked into a vine base, the bright green, heart-shaped leaves make a dramatic statement. Page 60 provides instructions for making the sedum wreath; the living ivy wreath can be found on page 59.

When you just can't resist picking up one more shell, and you find you have quite a collection by the end of the day, there is no easier way to display them than by making a wreath. Directions are on page 56.

With the summer months comes an abundance of flowers and herbs. The three projects illustrated here and the one on the following page demonstrate strikingly different ways to sustain the beauty of summer blossoms for many months to come. A portable bookshelf displays an entire bouquet of pressed flowers and foliage. Tiny herbs sparkle in the sunlight when preserved within beveled glass. More subtle, but no less beautiful, paper made from flower blossoms has a look and feel that is unique. When bound into a petal paper notebook, it becomes a lasting treasure. The sweet fragrance of roses can be worn close to your heart in a necklace made of rose petal beads. Directions for the bookshelf start on page 66, herbs under glass can be found on page 65, the petal paper notebook begins on page 61, and the rose petal necklace starts on page 55.

The Bamboo Window

see photo page 41

Intriguing and distinctive window play happens when hard-walled, hollow stems of naturally ringed bamboo are laced together to frame the delicate, swirling designs of translucent rice paper.

If you have never considered it before, you may want to think about planting some bamboo. A member of the grass family, bamboo is becoming increasingly popular as a house plant, and it is a favorite in the yard. Of the more than 700 species, only the giant cane is native to North America.

Artful to look at, and fascinating to make, this bamboo window measuring 24" x 24" quickly becomes a personal delight in creative design.

MATERIALS

    4 bamboo pieces, 24" x 1" diameter
    4 bolts, 2-1/4" x 3/16" diameter, with
        matching nuts
    4 bamboo pieces, 22" x 1/2" diameter
    1 piece of rice paper, 22" x 22"
    raffia
    glue
    masking tape
    pressed leaves from bamboo or willow
    pressed flower blossoms
    2 screw eyes
    2 bumper wall protectors (to cover the screw
        eyes)
    4 bumper wall protectors (to cover the nut
        and bolt ends)

TOOLS

    sharp knife
    electric drill with 3/16" bit
    hammer

INSTRUCTIONS

1. Drill a 3/16" hole 1-1/2" from the end of each 24" bamboo piece.

2. Overlay the top and bottom 24" horizontal pieces onto the side 24" pieces, and insert a 2-1/4" bolt in each corner, joining the four ends of the 1" diameter bamboo pieces. Secure the bolts with the matching nuts. Cover the hardware ends with bumper wall protectors.

3. Split the two 22" long (1/2" diameter) bamboo pieces in half by placing a sharp knife on top of one end. Tap the knife with a hammer, and the bamboo will split into two halves.

4. With the four bamboo halves, assemble the grid "panes." Make the center "pane" approximately 9-1/2" square.

5. Use raffia to cross-tie the joints of the grid and to do a figure-eight wrap on the corner joints of the 24" frame ends.

6. Place the bamboo frame on the floor, and slide the grid into place. The grid will secure itself firmly with the verticals and horizontals going over and under the frame.

7. Cut the rice paper into a square 22" x 22", and lay it flat on a table. Carefully glue leaves and flowers onto the rice paper, making a design that will look attractive through the grid.

8. With the grid and frame assembled, lay the entire window frame with the right side down, and temporarily tape the rice paper into place. The design should be facing through the window grid. Look at the design from the front, and check all of the edges. Tape or glue the rice paper permanently in place along the vertical frame members.

9. Attach the screw eyes on the back of the top horizontal frame piece. Place one screw eye about 1" in from each end of the frame. Press one bumper wall protector onto the end of each screw eye.

Raffia Summer Sandals

see photo page 40

Fiber sandals may be the most timeless, universal form of footwear that we're ever likely to encounter. Although inexpensive ones can be easily purchased in most areas of the country, here's a chance to experience some sandal-weaving artistry first hand.

The raffia fiber used to make these summer sandals comes from Madagascar palm leaves (the *Raphia ruffia* tree), and it is sold in bundles, ready for use, at most craft stores. Pliable, soft, and surprisingly strong, the long beige strips can easily be wrapped, lashed, knotted, and sewn together to make these sandals. The finished sandals are ideal for patio and beach wear.

MATERIALS

1 pound of raffia

TOOLS

1 large darning or blunt-tip needle
scissors
ruler

INSTRUCTIONS

1. To make the sole, gather 10 raffia strands of about equal length into a bunch. Place a single strand of raffia across the center of the bundle.

2. Wrap the single strand tightly around the bunch several times to start a coil.

3. Bend the wrapped section into a U-shape, and begin to join the two sides of the "U" with a figure-eight wrapping (see Figure 1).

4. Continue wrapping. This will form the core of the sandal (Figure 2).

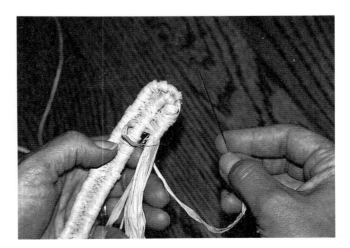

50

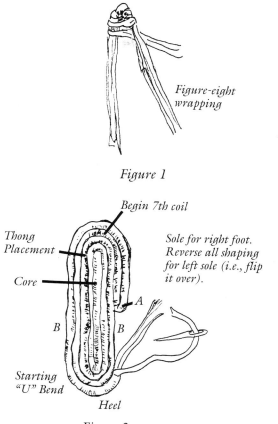

Figure-eight wrapping

Figure 1

Begin 7th coil

Thong Placement

Core

Sole for right foot. Reverse all shaping for left sole (i.e., flip it over).

A

B   B

Starting "U" Bend

Heel

Figure 2

5. When the core is 8" long (for a size 8 sandal) or 7" long (for a size 7, etc.), trim off the loose strands from one side of the core. Trim the right side for a right sole, or the left side for a left sole. Bring the other loose strands around the cut end, and thread one of these strands through your needle. Begin lashing the bunch of loose strands to the coil beside them, as shown in Figure 3.

6. Continue lashing. When you get near the end of the strands, attach ten more strands by overlapping the ends of the old and new pieces. Wrap this area several times with a single strand, and lash it to the coil beside it for reinforcement. Continue lashing.

7. When you get near the end of your lashing strand, run the end of it back through a coil on the underside of the sandal. Thread a new strand of raffia through a coil about 2" behind the point where your first strand ended, and continue lashing with the new strand.

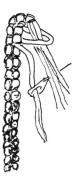

Figure 3

Figure-eight lashing

Figure 4

Figure-eight knotting

8. As you begin the seventh coil (see Figure 2), work halfway down the side of the sandal; then double back with your coil. Continue lashing until you come back around to meet the doubled bend. Trim away all but 1" of the loose strands and lash the ends to the outside coil at the doubled bend (point "A" in Figure 2). This completes the sole.

9. To make the thong (which goes between your first and second toes), gather eight to ten 8"-long strands into a bunch, and wrap a 1-1/2"-long coil. Bend the coil in half to make a loop, and wrap the ends together for an additional 1". Attach the thong in the position shown in Figure 2 by threading the loose strands (four at a time) down through the top of the sole. Cut off all but 5" from the ends of the raffia strands. Tie knots close to the underside of the sole, and anchor the ends by threading them through the coils.

10. Make the sandal strap by lashing two 8-strand bunches together with figure-eight knotting (see Figure 4).

11. Make ten to 15 knots spaced 1" apart along the strap.

12. Slip the strap through the thong loop, and try on the sandals. Pull the straps approximately to the points ("B") noted in Figure 2, and mark the most comfortable placement. After removing the sandals, attach the straps at the marked points by lashing the loose strap ends to the underside of the outer coils on both sides of each sole.

Blossom Bookmarks

see photo page 43

Many of the smallest wildflowers—some with blossoms no bigger than a small coin—are found in the brightest colors. The lasting beauty of wildflowers in gold, pink, purple, and blue will be highly visible when these flowers are used to create delicate designs on bookmarks. These blossom bookmarks are easy to make and inexpensive enough that you can make quite a few at a time; they make unforgettable personal gifts.

The first step in creating a pressed flower bookmark is, of course, to collect the flowers. Back yards, roadsides, and mountain meadows generally have an abundant selection of the petite and colorful blossoms, along with lacy leaves and delicate seedling grasses. There are literally hundreds of common small flowers ideal for pressing and framing; these include violets, chickweed, clover, mustard, goldenrod, hawkweed, asters, mint, buttercups, and many, many others. If none of these flowers is available for you to pick, you might want to try the craft stores and art stores that sell packets of pressed flowers.

Tiny seedling grasses and leaves are almost as important to pick as the flowers themselves. They will add delicacy and texture to the design.

MATERIALS

pressed flowers
Bristol board #280
glue (any latex-based adhesive)
polyurethane or varnish
colored cording

TOOLS

ruler
craft knife or razor
fine point pen
paper punch
tweezers
paintbrushes, #4 and #6
varnish brush, 1" wide
cutting board surface

INSTRUCTIONS

Collecting the Blossoms

1. Pick your wildflowers when the blossoms are as dry as possible. Cut the blossoms and their foliage with scissors to avoid pulling up any roots. Because many wildflowers wilt so quickly, make sure to take a pressing book with you when you venture out. For an immediate substitute for a pressing book, you can use two rectangles of cardboard with paper towels sandwiched between them.

2. Press the wildflowers with their stems and leaves. Gently pluck off the petals of flowers with hard centers. First press the petals; the whole flowers can be re-assembled later.

The drying time required for pressing depends on the condition of the flowers. Delicate wildflower pieces usually do not need more than a day or two. Never put the flowers in water once they have been picked.

3. Many dried flowers begin to fade. They can be touched up with watercolor paint. Dip your brush into a little liquid detergent before applying the paint. The detergent will make the flower pieces more absorbent and prevent the paint from running.

Making the Frame

4. A piece of Bristol board is used to make a mounting frame for your wildflower bookmark. To avoid cutting errors, make a pattern first, and trace it lightly on the board. A rectangular frame with outer dimensions of 6-5/8" x 1-3/4" makes a good size for a blossom bookmark. The side and bottom edges of the frame are 3/8" wide, and the top edge measures 3/4". This creates an interior space of 5-1/2" x 1".

5. To make straight, clean edges, use a craft knife or a razor blade. Always cut on a hard surface (such as a cutting board), and cut against the edge of a firmly held ruler. Be careful when cutting the inside corners of the frame. Press the blade down firmly to release any raw edges of the inside corners, and do not pull the board away before you have a complete cut. To avoid having sharp corners, you may want to round off the outer corners of your frame.

Creating the Design

6. Before starting your design, cut a piece of Bristol board to use as matting for the flowers. Cut the board 6" x 1-1/2". (It should be slightly smaller than the outer dimensions of the frame.)

7. Place selected flowers, leaves, and grass pieces onto the matting, experimenting with colors and designs. Select two or three buds as focal points, then fill in with smaller details. You might want to try mixing unlike flower centers and stems, or using the undersides of leaves and petals. Don't hesitate to lay one piece on top of another. In planning your design, leave the margins of the paper empty, so the paper will later fit flat against the frame.

8. When you are satisfied with the arrangement, slide the pieces off of the matting. Pour a dollop of latex adhesive onto a piece of heavy scrap paper. Using the glue sparingly, apply a spot of the adhesive on the corolla (the outer layer of petals) of a whole flower, on the top end of a single petal, or on the centers of smaller leaves. Grasses and stems need only be glued down at one or two points. For the very tiniest pieces you will need tweezers to tip the flower piece into the glue, and position it on the matting.

9. Excess latex adhesive can easily be removed by rubbing it off with your finger before it has had time to dry; this will leave no stain on the paper matting.

10. A clear plastic polyurethane or a varnish coating protects the design while allowing the creation to retain its three-dimensional appearance. Using a 1" brush, apply the coating over the design, moving from bottom to top. Leave the coated design on a flat surface to dry for about 40 minutes. Apply a second coat when the first is dry, and allow another 30 to 40 minutes of drying time.

11. Brush adhesive onto the back of the Bristol board frame and press it carefully and firmly on top of the varnished matting.

12. The bookmark will look more finished if you attach a colorful cord. Punch a hole at the top of the bookmark, insert a 6" length of colored cord, and fringe the cord ends.

13. To personalize your creation, choose a tiny and perfect blossom to glue in the lower left corner of the border as a signature blossom. In the lower right corner, sign your name with a fine-line marker.

Rose Petal Necklace
Sweet-Smelling Beads from Roses
see photo page 48

In the late sixteenth century, beads made from rose petals were strung into rosaries. The worshiper's warm hand intensified the fragrance of the beads. Through the years a rose bead necklace often held great sentimental value because it was made with roses from grandmother's garden or from a bride's bouquet. Delicately colored and scented, a rose bead necklace is still a romantic accessory.

You too can master this heavenly scented craft. You simply take rose petals that are past their prime, and make them into a paste. From the paste, you fashion some sweet-smelling beads. A rose bead necklace carries its perfume for months, revived by the warmth of body heat when it is worn.

Once the beads are finished, they can be strung any number of ways. They mix equally well with semi-precious stones or nuggets, silver or gold beads, and even with glass beads.

MATERIALS

    enough rose petals to fill a shopping bag*
    rose oil or unscented vegetable oil
    clear monofilament (fishing line) or waxed
       dental floss
    jewelry clasp
    semi-precious stone beads (optional)

TOOLS

    large sewing needle
    meat grinder or scissors
    enamel or cast iron pot
    wooden spoon
    large shaft stick pins
    basket lid or corkboard
    soft cloth

Makes about 40 to 60 beads, depending on size.

INSTRUCTIONS

Use the most fragrant roses you can find, and pick them in the early morning on a sunny, warm day. At that hour, and in newly opened roses, the fragrant oils are most concentrated.

The best roses to use for this project are the old-fashioned standbys such as *Rosa centifolia*, the cabbage rose; *Rosa gallica*, the French rose, and *Rosa damascena*, the damask rose.

1. Tear the rose petals into small pieces, and put them through a meat grinder to form a clay-like substance.

2. Grind the petals into either a cast-iron skillet or an enameled pan. Any other pans will turn black if they come in contact with crushed rose petals. Leave the petals uncovered as you grind more. The ground petals should have the consistency of a paste.

3. If a meat grinder is not available, put the petals into a stainless steel saucepan, barely covered with water. Heat them to just below the simmering point for one hour, but do not let them boil. After heating, let them cool and stand for 24 hours. Repeat this procedure three more times. For the final heating, add one teaspoon of ground cinnamon and one teaspoon of ground cloves. The petals should now be a smooth paste.

4. Rub your hands with rose oil or unscented vegetable oil. Pinch off about 1/4 teaspoon (more or less depending on the size bead you desire) of petal paste and roll it between the palms of your hand to form a bead.

5. The beads will shrink as they dry, so make each bead twice the desired finished size.

6. Push a pin through the center of each bead while it is still moist. Stick the pin, with the bead on it, into either a basket lid or a piece of cork-board so that the air can circulate around the bead. Make 40 to 60 beads using this process. Allow the beads to dry for three to four days.

7. When the beads are completely dry, rub each bead with rose oil, and polish each one with a soft cloth.

8. String the beads on dental floss or monofilament. Alternate the beads with semi-precious stones if you wish. Continue to add beads until your necklace is the length that you want. Attach a jewelry clasp to finish the necklace.

If the fragrance fades after several months, it can be renewed by rubbing the beads with rose oil.

Seashell Wreath
see photo page 45

Glistening in the summer sun, a treasured collection of seashells, sought or bought, makes a fascinating natural wreath to hang at the cottage door, on the deck, or on an office wall.

Create an intriguing wreath arrangement of incredible shapes and colors using seashells, tiny crab shells, and even starfish. Glue your collection onto layered vine wreaths, creating a dimensional design that emerges as each shell is fitted and placed into, over, and around the vines that twist from the outside to the center of the wreath.

MATERIALS

> 2 vine wreaths (wisteria, grapevine, or other sturdy vine), one smaller than the other
> seashells, all sizes
> small twists of driftwood
> picture wire

TOOLS

> glue gun

INSTRUCTIONS

1. The smaller of the two wreaths should just fit on the inside edges of the larger vine wreath, giving the assembly a deep, dimensional look. Glue the two wreaths together with the outer edges of the inside wreath resting on the inner edges of the larger wreath.

2. Sort your shell collection by grouping like sizes and kinds. Set aside special pieces so that they are available for specific locations.

3. Glue and place the shells around the vine wreaths, one overlapping another. Fill in small, vacant spots with tiny shells and interesting drift-wood pieces.

4. At the center back of the wreath, find a strong twist of vines, and insert the picture wire. Twist and turn the wire into a hanging loop.

Seashell Wind Chimes

see photo page 43

Seashells turning in the wind are a pleasant reminder of the seashore. Sixteen scallop shells—threaded into three dangling chains—make this tinkling, twisting wind chime. It is secured at the top by a weathered piece of driftwood.

Scallops, sundials, or sea urchin spines make delightful and wondrous wind chimes. Each type of shell has its own sound depending on its size, shape, and configuration. Wind chimes made with just one type of shell make an especially harmonious sound when they touch one another in the wind.

Scallops can be found almost everywhere there are beaches. Don't despair if you don't live near a beach, though; scallop and other shells are readily available in craft and seashell stores.

Likewise, it is not necessary to have a beach nearby to find interesting pieces of wood. Weathered wood or partially decayed tree roots strongly resemble driftwood and can often be found during a stroll through the woods.

MATERIALS

> 20 scallop or other shells
> driftwood or weathered wood
> dental floss or monofilament line

TOOLS

> electric drill with 1/16" bit
> needle
> scissors

INSTRUCTIONS

1. Drill a tiny hole at least 1/4" down from the top edge, and on the inside, of each shell. Be sure to hold the shell firmly on a piece of wood, drilling through the shell and into the wood. Shells are very fragile, and drilling holes in them takes extreme care.

2. Arrange the shells on a table or the floor so that the edges will touch each other when they turn. Design how you want each chain of shells to hang (i.e., one long chain and two shorter ones).

Experiment to determine the best design; shells of different sizes make different sounds.

3. With a threaded needle in hand, begin by guiding the monofilament or floss through the hole at the top of the last shell in the chain. Secure the shell in place with a knot; then move from shell to shell, tying and knotting at each shell hole. When all of the shells on one chain have been attached, pass the thread through a hole in the drift wood.

4. Similarly, thread and knot the rest of the shells into the remaining two chains. Pass the threads through holes in the driftwood, and tie all three threads together. Glue the threads in place on top of the driftwood, and cover the threads with one large shell or several small shells glued to the driftwood.

A Fish Print Story

see photos page 42

Fishing is family fun—a time for getting out the fishing poles, digging worms, collecting bait, packing a snack, and getting in the boat. Then cast off, and head out to sea (or onto the nearest fishing lake) to catch the biggest and best fish. That's usually the fish that gets into print.

Here are two kinds of fish prints to try. To make the Japanese-style fish print, you will paint a fresh fish with India ink and transfer the shape and texture onto rice paper. A different effect can be achieved using tempera paint and a roller.

MATERIALS

1 fresh fish (whole)
1 piece of rice paper larger than the fish
India ink
tempera paint, any color (optional)
1 piece of backing (plywood, pressed board, or heavy poster board) larger than the fish
liquid gesso
polymer medium
waxed paper

TOOLS

1" foam throw-away paint brush
#3 retouching brush
small paint roller (optional)

INSTRUCTIONS

1. First cover your working surface with waxed paper. Then place the fish on the waxed paper.

2. Using the foam throw-away brush, liberally cover the better side of the fish with India ink.

3. Lay the rice paper lightly over the fish, and press the paper firmly against the fish until all of the important features show through the rice paper. Once the transfer is made, use care while removing the rice paper, or your print may smudge.

4. With the imprinted side facing up, set the rice paper on a flat surface. Let it dry thoroughly.

Now is the time to retouch any important details that may be missing. Use your retouching brush moistened with a little of the ink.

5. Before mounting the print on the backing (plywood, pressed board, or heavy posterboard), gently tear away the excess rice paper from around the imprint. Cover the surface of the backing with gesso.

6. Press the fish print in place on the backing, using your hands to press out any air bubbles. After the print has dried thoroughly, carefully brush the entire fish print with polymer medium (a light varnish).

For added interest, you can enhance your fish print with other colors to make the fish look more realistic.

Alternative Printing Method

7. For a less permanent fish imprint, use a soft, small roller to paint the fish with your favorite color of tempera. When the fish is covered liberally, lay the fish—painted side down—onto your paper. Carefully remove the fish, and let the print dry. Trim the edges of the paper, and mount the print as described above.

A Living Wreath
For All Seasons

see photo page 44

The wreath is a well-known symbol of hospitality, and the vine denotes longevity. The combination—a living wreath made from lengths of vine—provides a generous welcome indoors or out. It is just the right size to hang on a 30" door, and it is equally attractive on a deck railing, on a front porch column, over the mantel, or on the wall above a buffet.

The wreath in these photos was made with woodvine, which grows abundantly in the Northwest woods near my home. You are likely to find this or similar vines growing along the ground and climbing into the trees in the woods in your area. Wild grapevine that is a few years old works very well. The knobs, bends, and twists of the vine give the wreath its intriguing shape; they also create pockets in which you can place small plants for live greenery, or seasonal decorations such as dried flowers and fall leaves.

MATERIALS

3 lengths of vine, approximately 1" diameter
8 small ivy plants or rooted cuttings
sheet moss
potting soil
spool of dark thread

TOOLS

clippers
scissors

INSTRUCTIONS

1. Starting with one long, thick length of vine, cross the ends over one another to form a circle approximately 22" in diameter. Grasping the crossover point with one hand, use your other hand to pull one end of the vine through the middle of the circle. Wrap it to the outside and then up through the center again, making long spirals with the vine. Repeat this wrapping procedure with the other end of the vine. Secure the ends simply by tucking them into the small gaps.

2. Experiment with the additional lengths by adding a second round of wrapping to the wreath you have made. Try coiling the full length of one vine into a 22" circle, then wrapping a second vine around that. Try combining two or three wreaths of descending size.

3. Once the vine is twisted, its irregularities create pockets that become the site of attachment for a variety of seasonal decorations. Through the summer, you can have small, living plants that will create an ever-changing look for your wreath. For fall, decorate it with pastiches of dried flowers, herbs, and clusters of bronzed leaves. During the holiday season, fill the twists in the basic vine wreath with pine and holly branches, bells, and bright red plaid ribbon.

Plants for the Living Wreath

4. Choose small house plants such as ivy or philodendron for a wreath that is to hang indoors. Purchase the smallest size sold in stores, or root your own clippings. House plants will flourish for six to eight months before outgrowing the wreath. At that time, they can be transplanted to pots and the wreath refilled.

5. For an outdoor display, English ivy *(Hedera helix)* is ideal. It comes in many varieties with differently shaped leaves of green or variegated green and white. For best results choose a variety that flourishes where you live.

A wreath made with English ivy can hang outdoors all year round. Where winters are snowy and cold, it's best to take the plants from the wreath and set them into the yard in the fall. Fill the wreath with newly rooted cuttings the following spring.

6. The living wreath will hold about eight small ivy plants. To grow your own rooted plants, place cuttings in a tinted glass container kept out of the sun. Two inches of coarse sand or pebbles in the bottom of the container will hold the stems firm and encourage rooting. It takes about a month for roots to form.

Planting

7. To prepare the cuttings for insertion into the wreath, you will need a large package of sheet moss and some good potting soil with a high humus content. (Sheet moss is available from suppliers of orchid and tropical plant material.)

8. Take the dry moss out of the packet, spray it with water and spread it out on a flat surface. Gently tear away a square of moss about 6" on each side, and spoon some soil mix into the center. Insert the plant roots into the soil, making sure that the roots are covered. Firm the soil around the plant, up to the stems and leaves.

9. By folding the dampened moss firmly around the soil and plant, you will create a miniature balled plant. The ball must be securely wrapped using strong, dark buttonhole thread.

Have the spool upright so that the thread feeds out easily, leaving your hands free to do the wrapping. A good method to hold the spool is to tap a 3" nail through its center hole into a small board.

Wrap each balled plant securely, turning the ball as you wrap. Place the balled and wrapped plant in a few inches of water to soak.

10. Determine which part of the wreath should be the top, then stand it upright on a table against a supporting wall. Then "pocket" the plants into the best openings. Squeeze water into the center of each plant's root ball once or twice or week to keep the soil and surrounding moss moist.

11. With some gentle persuasion and a little time, your plants will flourish, creating a long-lasting symbol of growth and renewal.

The Growing Sedum Wreath

see photo page 44

A wreath made with live sedums can almost be more theatrical than nature allows. The ever-blooming sedums spread to become intriguing live productions in a constantly changing wreath scene of fascinating textures and flowers. Carpeted in moisture-loving moss, a 12" wire wreath makes an excellent base for four or five plant varieties to grow together.

MATERIALS

 4 or 5 varieties of sedum
 12" wire wreath
 dried moss
 fertilizer (fish fertilizer is best)
 monofilament line

TOOLS

 scissors

INSTRUCTIONS

1. Pack moss into the wire wreath, pressing the moss firmly into place, until the wreath is filled.

2. Shake some fertilizer lightly into the moss.

3. Wrap the monofilament around the entire moss-filled wreath to prevent the moss from coming loose. Then water the wreath thoroughly.

4. Insert the blades of your scissors into the moss, and twist the scissors to create a hole large enough to hold a sedum. Take one sedum and plant it in the hole. Plant the remaining sedums at various points around the wreath, leaving room around the plants for them to spread.

5. Lay the wreath in a place where it can be watered every day for two weeks. The sedums will take hold easily.

6. After the sedums have established a footing, hang the wreath on a deck, porch wall, or fence, and watch the sedum scene change.

Handmade Petal Paper—
"Nature's Notebook"
see photos page 47

The basic method for forming paper fiber hasn't changed in almost two thousand years. You can make paper today using plants and household things the same way that the Chinese made the first paper approximately 100 years after the birth of Christ.

To be classed as true paper, the individual sheets must be made from fiber that has been mashed until each filament is a separate unit. The fibers are mixed with water; then, with the use of a sieve-like screen, the "mash" is lifted from the water in the form of a thin sheet of matted fiber on the screen's surface. This thin layer of fiber is paper.

Using flowering plants from your backyard, and tools from your kitchen, you can make your own textured "petal paper." In late summer and early fall, many flower petals are ready for paper-making. If you don't have a flowering backyard, ask nurseries and florists for leftover blossoms. Plants ideally suited for blender papermaking include: cattail flowers, peonies, hydrangeas, gladiolas, and nasturtiums.

This pretty blossom-paper notebook was made from hydrangea petals and recycled paper mixed together in the kitchen blender. Poured from the blender into a dishpan, and floated onto a screened mold (mold and deckle), this simple method produces paper one sheet at a time.

MATERIALS
Petal Paper:
    fresh flower petals
    recycled paper or paper towels
Notebook:
    3 sheets 6" x 8" petal paper
    1 sheet 4" x 6" petal paper
    3 sheets 6" x 8" rice paper
    1 sheet 4" x 6" rice paper
    2 sheets 6" x 8" decorative lining paper
    2 strips 1-1/2"-wide white cloth tape
    2 pieces 5" split bamboo (purchase at nursery)

    white cotton string (good quality)
    24 sheets of quality writing paper cut to
      5-3/4" x 7-3/4"

TOOLS
Petal Paper:
    mold and deckle (to make one, see
      instructions, last paragraph)
    scissors or clippers
    measuring cup
    blender
    kitchen sink
    plastic dishpan large enough to hold the mold
    8 pieces of absorbent fabric (small terry cloth
      towels)
Notebook:
    scissors
    paper cutter
    yarn needle (for sewing with string)
    glue gun
    tacky glue
    hand drill with 1/8" bit

INSTRUCTIONS
Petal Paper
1. Cut the flower petals and recycled paper (paper towel) into 1" to 2" pieces. For a rough texture, make your paper using more plant petal material than recycled paper. A combination of half plant materials, half recycled paper produces a smooth-textured paper.

2. Fill your blender half-full with water. Starting on low speed, begin adding small amounts of paper and petals. Then mix at a fast speed for a short time. Stop every few seconds to make sure that the pulp is moving freely, and add more material until you have the paper and petals well blended.

3. Pour all of the blended pulp (the contents of four to six blenders) into your plastic dishpan container, and stir. This is your paper pulp.

4. Holding your mold and deckle level, dip them into the pulp mixture and move back and forth, going from the side nearest you to the opposite side (away from you).

Hold the mold and deckle steady; then lift them straight up out of the water. A thin layer of the pulp will be on the screen. If the pulp seems too thin, dip it back in again and repeat. As your mixture gets thinner, add more pulp a little at a time.

5. Hold the mold and deckle over the pulp mixture to let the excess water drip back into the container. Lift the deckle off the mold, and turn the mold over—paper side down—onto a damp towel. Gently lift the mold (tapping the screen is sometimes necessary), leaving the paper on the fabric. If the paper tears, put it back in the pulp mixture, and do it over again.

The paper may take a few moments to drop off the screen. If it seems too thin, push the paper sheet off the screen, back into the pulp, and add more pulp to the mixture.

6. Add decorative petals to the top side of the paper, and dribble a few teaspoons of pulp over the petals to hold them securely until the paper is dry.

7. Layer three to six sheets of paper, each on a piece of fabric, on top of one another. Press your own weight or a large book onto the stack, squeezing out any excess water.

After pressing, remove the top fabric, and gently lift the sheet of paper off the fabric. Paper is delicate at this point; put it back into the blender if it tears.

8. Gently smooth each sheet of paper onto a flat, glass surface to dry (a glass sliding door or picture window is ideal). Allow the sheets of paper to dry thoroughly for at least 24 hours, and peel each sheet away from the glass. The glass-dried side of the paper will be the shiny side of each sheet.

Note: You can use a hair dryer to speed up the drying process.

A Petal Paper Notebook

9. Lay out three sheets of petal paper for book covers (see Figure 1).

10. Measure and cut two pieces of cloth tape 6" long. These form the notebook's hinges that connect the three book covers into one long, 3-piece, 3-fold book cover.

11. Now cut two strips of petal paper 1-1/4" wide. Glue the paper strips over the cloth tape hinges on the outside of the book cover.

12. Next, cut two strips of rice paper 1-1/4" to fit over the hinges on the inside of the book cover.

13. Measure and cut three pieces of rice paper to cover the inside of the cover sheets. Glue them in place carefully with tacky glue.

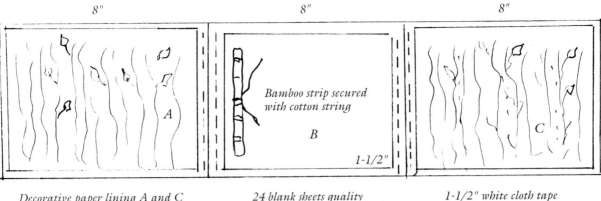

8"   8"   8"

Decorative paper lining A and C

Bamboo strip secured
with cotton string

B

1-1/2"

24 blank sheets quality
writing paper attached
to inside center panel.

1-1/2" white cloth tape
overlapping back hinges
between A - B and B - C.

Length of 3 panels opened is 24-3/4".

Figure 1

14. Then cut two pieces of decorative lining paper the same size as the cover sheets. Glue the decorative sheets in place on the inside (rice paper side) of the two outer cover sheets ("A" and "C" in Figure 1).

15. Cut 24 sheets of quality writing paper to fit on the inside of the middle cover (sheet "B" in Figure 1).

16. To make holes through the sheets of writing paper, first mark two holes (horizontally) near the upper left corner of the papers. As shown in Figure 2, the holes should be 1/2" apart, 1/2" in from the left edge of the paper, and 3/4" down from the top. Mark a second pair of holes at the center of the page, placing them 1/2" apart and in line with the first pair. Mark a third pair of holes 3/4" from the bottom of the page, placing them in line with the others.

Holding the 24 sheets of paper firmly against a straight edge, drill holes through the markings.

17. Thread a yarn needle with the white cotton string. Then position one strip of bamboo on the front side of the pages before you begin lacing.

Push the threaded needle (from the front) down through the right center hole, leaving a 4" end of the string hanging loose (to be used as a tie later). Bring the needle up through the right top hole, cross over the bamboo, and down through the left top hole. Push the needle up through the left center hole, cross over the bamboo piece, and go down through the right center hole. Thread up through the right bottom hole, cross over the bamboo, and come back up through the left center hole. Cut the string to match the free end, tie the two strings together into a knot, and leave the loose ends dangling.

Sewing the string over the bamboo in this pattern makes a neat design of string lacing on the back cover (see Figure 2 showing the back of sheet "B").

Back of closed book.

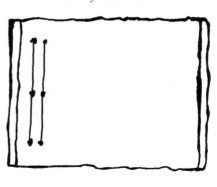

Figure 2

18. Place the other piece of split bamboo 1" in from the outer edge of the top cover page. Glue the bamboo in place, and loop a string firmly over it (see the pattern in Figure 3).

19. Fold back the right end cover to the inside, over the sheets of writing paper. Fold the top cover (left page) over everything.

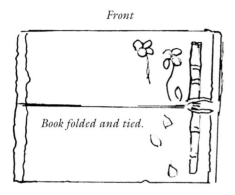

Front

Book folded and tied.

Folding: C folds over B, then A folds over C.

Figure 3

Mold and Deckle

It is quite simple to construct a mold and deckle, even if you have never made one before. The mold is a frame with screen attached, and the deckle is a second frame that holds the pulp onto the mold until the pulp becomes a sheet ready to be placed onto a towel.

MATERIALS

3/4" x 3/4" white pine, 72" long
stainless steel staples
2" coated finishing nails
nylon window screening, 30 or 40 mesh

TOOLS

saw
T-square
hammer
staple gun

INSTRUCTIONS

1. In order to get a 6" x 8" (interior dimensions) mold, cut two 6" lengths and two 9-1/2" pieces of white pine. Be sure the corners are cut square.

2. Place the shorter lengths inside the longer ones, and staple the four corners on both faces of the frame. Firm up the joints with a 2" finishing nail at each corner (use coated nails for a better hold).

3. Next lay the screen over the edges of the frame, and secure the screen firmly with staples. Try to avoid any wrinkles. Staple the screen with a staple gun, putting staples approximately 1" apart around all four sides of the frame. Pull the screen snug at the corners. This screened frame is the mold.

4. Make a second, identical frame but without a screen. The unscreened frame is the deckle.

Herbs Under Beveled Glass
A Framed Herb Garden

see photo page 46

Herbs have been grown and used for culinary, medicinal, and cosmetic purposes for generations. In fact, evidence gained from inscriptions on stones and clay tablets indicates that the ancient Chinese, Indians, and Egyptians developed a vast number of herbal remedies.

Delicate herbs—framed in glass to hang in a kitchen window—turn round and round, playing in the light from all angles. Beveled edges cause the glass to sparkle, enhancing the intriguing leaf and flower designs. You need no experience with glass to be able to make a beveled glass window hanging, and you can make any of these designs in less than an hour.

MATERIALS

    2 pieces of beveled glass for each hanging frame, 2" x 6" rectangles or 3" x 5" ovals
copper foil tape 1/4" wide
solder
flux
pressed herbs or small flowers
galvanized wire, about 2" for each design

TOOLS

    soldering iron
glass cleaner and lint-free rag
steel wool, 000 (optional)
tinner's fluid, black (optional)

INSTRUCTIONS

1. Ideally, one should cut and press the herbs at mid-morning on a sunny day, just as their flowers begin to open. Choose herbs like the delicate chive blossom, lovage, bronze fennel, lavender, and dill to press and frame.

2. Clean the beveled glass thoroughly with glass cleaner and the lint-free rag.

3. Peel off enough copper foil tape to completely fit around the piece of glass. Remove the adhesive backing from the foil, and center the edge of the glass in the width of the foil. There must be an equal width of overhang on both sides of the glass. If the tape does not overlap equally on both sides, take off the tape and put down a new piece. Secure the foil tape on the beveled or sloped side of the glass piece only. Be as neat as possible, laying the glass pieces flat on your work table and burnishing the foil so that it will be smooth and tight.

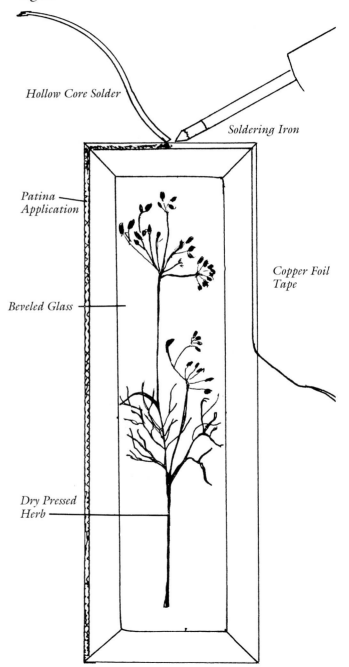

Hollow Core Solder

Soldering Iron

Patina Application

Copper Foil Tape

Beveled Glass

Dry Pressed Herb

4. Position the herb (or flower) on the flat side of the taped glass, and place the flat side of a second piece of glass (which is not taped at this point) down over the flower. Match the edges of the taped glass and the untaped glass perfectly, with the bevels facing out. Hold the two pieces together firmly, and fold the tape smoothly down onto the second bevel.

5. Brush flux on the exposed copper foil surrounding the glass, one piece at a time. Holding the soldering iron over the copper foil, bring the end of the solder wire to the tip of the iron. Move both the wire and the iron continuously around the edges of the glass along the center or bend of the foil. The hot solder will follow the iron, flowing over the copper foil in an even coating.

6. To make a hanger for the glass pieces, cut a 1-1/2" to 2" length of galvanized wire and bend it to form a small loop. Decide how you want to hang the beveled glass, and position the loop accordingly. Brush on flux, and solder the wire hanger in place.

7. Clean the glass pieces thoroughly with glass cleaner and the lint-free cloth. For a silver patina finish, buff the soldered seams with 000 steel wool. If you want a dull grey to black patina, brush tinner's fluid onto the solder with a cotton swab. Any of the fluid that spills onto the glass must be wiped up immediately.

Portable "Bouquet" Bookshelf

see photo page 46

The old saying "books in daily use should be conveniently kept" led to the idea and design for this pretty, portable bookshelf. A handy addition to a desk or table top, it measures 20" from end to end, and stands 9" high.

Its bouquet-shaped ends are beautifully covered with pressed and dried flower blossoms and leaves. It is sealed with a glossy lacquer and finished with a gold ribbon tied at the base.

MATERIALS

> 1 piece of 1 x 10 clear white pine, 36" long
> (*Note: The actual dimensions of a 1 x 10 are 3/4" x 9-3/4"*)
> 1 piece of 2-1/2" x 3/4" hardwood (oak, walnut, etc.), 36" long
> 4 small angle shelf brackets, 1" x 1"
> 1/2" flathead wood screws
> pressed flowers
> gold acrylic paint
> glossy lacquer or varnish
> gold ribbon

TOOLS

> electric jigsaw or hand coping saw
> 2 "C" clamps or wood clamps
> sandpaper
> #6 paint brush

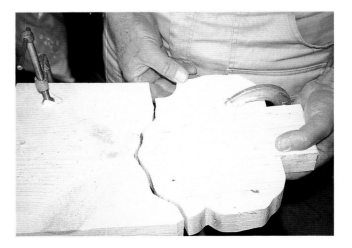

INSTRUCTIONS

1. Cut one 12" piece from the 36" length of pine (leaving a 24" piece).

2. Place the 12" piece on top of the 24" piece, matching the edges and square one end perfectly.

3. Clamp the two pieces together using "C" clamps or wood clamps. Copy the pattern of the bookshelf end piece onto a clear (no knots) section of the 12" piece.

4. Nail the long end of the 24" piece to a work table or saw horse, permitting you to saw both of the clamped pieces (together) at the same time.

5. Saw slowly, and take your time, particularly during the turns in the pattern. When you are finished sawing, you will have two identical bookshelf ends.

6. Sand the edges lightly.

7. Cut the 36" hardwood board in half to make two shelves, each 18" long.

8. Attach the shelves at a 90° angle to each other using 1" angle brackets at each end (see the illustration). It is important to get a center line of balance for the books. First establish a center line; then, using a framing square or a book, mark off a 90° angle with the center of the angle at the bottom. To maintain a proper weight balance, the "back" shelf bracket must be higher and a few (8 or 10) degrees more vertical than the "front" shelf bracket. The shelves do not touch at the bottom. Be sure to mark both bookshelf ends identically.

9. Paint both sides of both bookshelf ends with gold acrylic paint. Let them dry completely.

10. Glue an arrangement of blossoms and leaves onto the outsides of both bookshelf ends, and let them dry in place. Finish your bouquet bookshelf by brushing on a coat of lacquer and tying a gold ribbon at the base.

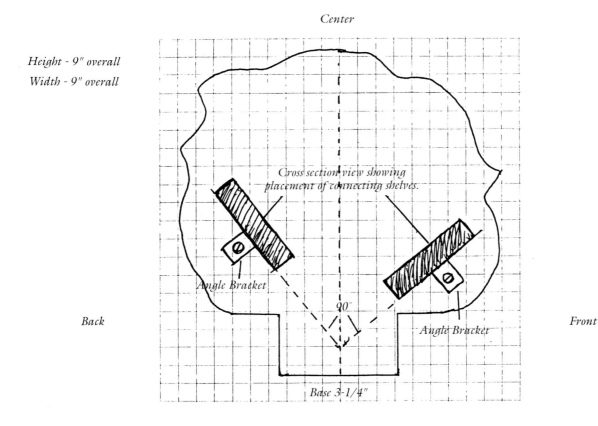

Center

Height - 9" overall
Width - 9" overall

Cross section view showing placement of connecting shelves.

Angle Bracket

90°

Back

Angle Bracket

Front

Base 3-1/4"

To Scale: 1 square = 3/8"

Twig Sketching Pencil

see photo page 40

A pencil is defined as a narrow cylindrical instrument for marking, consisting of a thin rod of graphite encased in wood. Nature's twig pencil is made from a cylindrical piece of wood cut from the branch of a tree. With its center hollowed, a rod of graphite is inserted securely, the end is sharpened, and this twig pencil is ready to write! A clutch of these naturally shaped pencils makes a novel gift.

MATERIALS

> twigs cut from willow, alder, or other tree, each 8–10" long
> coat hanger wire, 10" long
> graphite (large, art store variety)
> glue

TOOLS

> knife or clippers

INSTRUCTIONS

1. Cut three or four (or more) twig pieces from a tree branch. Choose straight pieces or some with interesting twists and bends.

2. Insert a 10" length of wire (bent 90° at one end to give you a better hand grip) into the end of a twig, twisting the wire as it goes into the pulp center. Withdraw the wire frequently to remove loosened pulp.

3. Make certain that you make a hole deep enough to accommodate your length of graphite. Cover the piece of graphite with tacky glue, and push the graphite into the opening made with the wire.

4. Let the glue dry; then sharpen your twig pencil with a sharp knife.

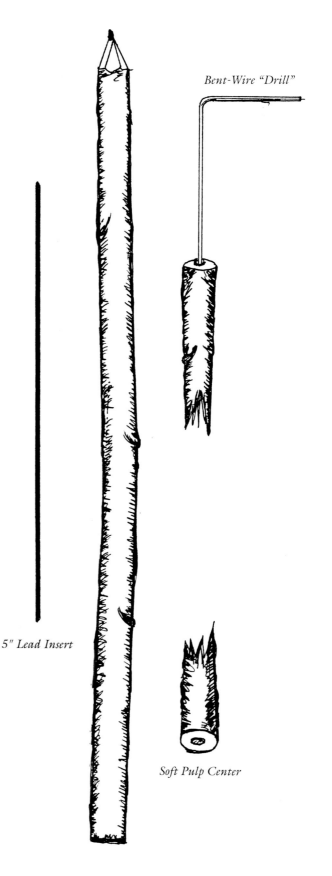

Bent-Wire "Drill"

5" Lead Insert

Soft Pulp Center

68

Refreshingly cool after the hot summer sunshine, autumn arrives with its own bright splash of color.

Cattails now going to seed are the perfect building materials for an English country bird-cage. Alone or holding a leafy plant, the steepled cage makes a handsome accent for the home. Instructions begin on page 79.

Hydrangea blossoms acquire a rosy golden hue in autumn, and late-blooming Sweet Annie can be found in many woodland settings. Each is perfect for creating an enchanting, heart-shaped wreath. Both wreaths are described on page 87.

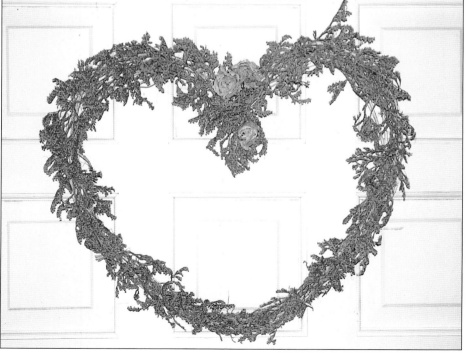

Using fresh-fallen leaves as your palette, an autumn leaf painting makes a striking statement. Directions are on page 86.

A family of goose decoys can be an afternoon project for the whole family. You need only a fistful of cattail stems, a piece of balsa wood, and a sharp knife to make each one. See page 84 for instructions.

Fall is one of the best times to collect vines for weaving into baskets of all shapes and dimensions. Use this wallflower basket to over-winter a favorite plant from the garden, or plant it with an interesting assortment of houseplants. Directions start on page 82.

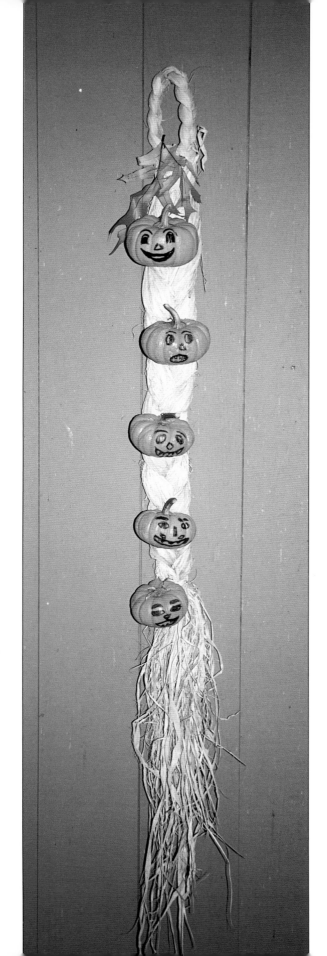
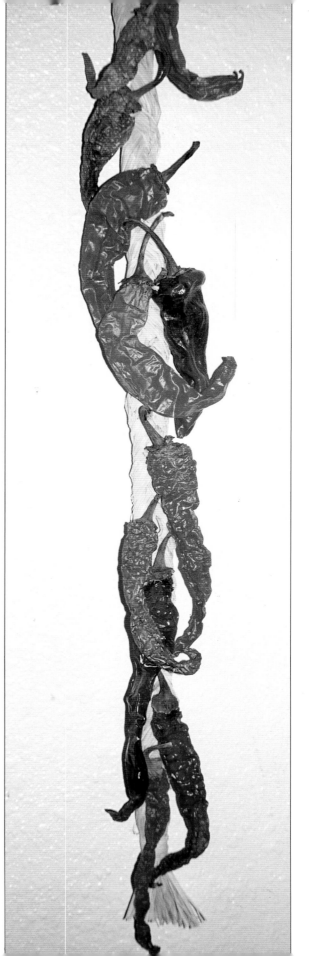

74

A fat, braided rope made from raffia offers an interesting and convenient way to display some of the season's bountiful harvest. Miniature pumpkins painted with jack-o-lantern faces can be hung at the door to greet young trick-or-treaters. In the kitchen, an assortment of cayenne peppers adds a spot of color as the peppers dry naturally. Instructions for the pumpkin braid begin on page 92, and the peppers are described on page 90.

This dramatic wreath mirror is made with pepper berry branches and bits of moss that you can collect on an afternoon hike through the woods. Directions start on page 91.

Projects for fall abound with a variety of natural materials. Honeysuckle vines make a charming basket to hold candy or small guest soaps. Paper ribbon curved into a pumpkin shape can nearly fool Mother Nature. Perfect for the child in all of us are tiny toy chairs built of cattail stems and finished with woven seats. An autumn gourd becomes an elegant box to hold ribbons or jewelry. Directions for the vine basket start on page 89, the paper pumpkins are on page 94, the toy chairs can be found on page 88, and page 95 describes the golden gourd.

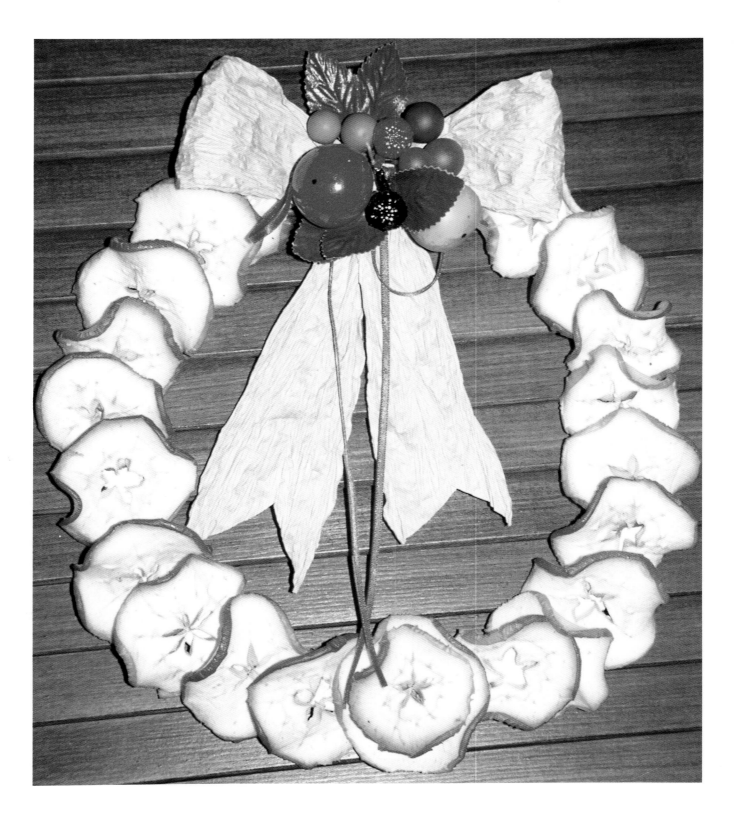

English Country Birdcage

see photo page 70

In the 18th century, country people in England would hang a birdcage like this cattail cage just outside their front door. It was their way of keeping a blackbird or starling nearby to sing for them. A little platform covered with a piece of turf held worms for the bird to eat.

For those who live in town, a birdcage, like a leafy potted plant, is a gentle reminder of the countryside.

You can make this country birdcage yourself from slender, sturdy cattails using the stem without the thick brown seed head. This long stem of the cattail looks and feels much like bamboo. It is light in weight and has intermittent ridges along the stem where the leaves grow.

Begin looking for the cattail stems after the first heavy frost; by then they will be fully mature and will have reached maximum size and strength. Work your hands to the base of the stalk, and with a sharp knife, begin cutting as near to the base as you can. Cut approximately 50 of the stalks.

You will be using the upper portion of the stems for this birdcage. Break off the brown "downy" flower heads, and save these heads in a bag or basket for other projects.

Take the stalks home with you where you can strip off all of the outer leaves and papery sheath coverings, leaving only the hard timber core. Use a knife to make several slices along the length of the stalk. This procedure makes it very easy to peel off the outer portions of the cattail.

Store the satiny brown timber stems in a dry place until they are completely dry. This curing process will keep the wood from shrinking or loosening after you have worked with it.

Before using the stems, sand them slightly to remove the stringy bark pieces and the rough spots where leaves were attached. The slimmer, top stems will be halved to make the birdcage. Cutting is easiest with a craft knife or razor-blade knife. Lay the stem on a cutting board and press the blade through the length of the stem. It takes 52 of these halved stems to make the birdcage.

MATERIALS

cattail stems
#2 reed
raffia
posterboard

TOOLS

scissors
sharp knife

INSTRUCTIONS

Note: Keep the cattail stems and #2 reed dampened while making the birdcage. Refer to the illustration for doing the twining weave.

1. On a flat working area, lay the 52 stakes (the split half-stems) parallel to each other, and hold them in place with a heavy board.

2. With a length of #2 reed bent in half, begin at the first stake to do a twining weave, going at a right angle from the first stake to the last (52nd). Place your weaving 1" down from the ends of the stakes.

3. Now bring the two ends (1st and 52nd stakes) together by twining them. This first row is the beginning of your birdcage, and it establishes the location of the base.

4. Continue your twining weave for the next six rows. Your stakes should be about a 1/2" apart, resulting in a base that is about 13" in diameter.

5. Gently flare the stakes to a spacing of approximately 1". Then take another length of reed, bend it in half, and begin twining about 8" above the first row of your weaving. Twine another two rows.

Remember to keep the stakes and reed dampened to maintain their flexibility. You can soak them in a tub, or hose them periodically to keep them wet.

6. At the center of the cage—about 4" above the last two rows of twining—twine two rows as before. Then make six rows of "double over and under weaving." This is simply using two parallel weavers as one. (See the illustration.)

7. Weave over and under for about 1-1/2". Then you are ready to upsett—to dampen the stakes (stems) and bend them inward to form the steeple-shaped top of the cage.

8. Pinch or lightly bend each stake at about the same place. The height from the first row of twining at the base to this upsett point is about 14". From bottom to top, the overall cage measures approximately 30".

9. Now weave (twine) two stakes as one. Do this twining for one row, at 5" above the upsett. At a point 2" up from this row, twine another row, again going over the two stakes (stems) as one.

10. Going in one direction around the birdcage, cut off every other stake (stem) and slip the ends of the cut stems under the uncut stems.

11. Again twine over two stakes as one, further decreasing the diameter of the top of the birdcage. The steeple top will end with 14 (two as one) stakes to weave.

12. Ease the single stakes together, close the ends to form the top of the steeple. Again (as at the cage center) weave four rows of the "double over and under" using two parallel weavers as one. These rows will be about 4" above the last single-twined row.

Binding the Stakes

13. Using a twisted weaver, make a circular loop for a handle (a hang-loop of twisted vines or reed). Slip the hang-loop onto another reed that has been bent in half, resting the loop at the bend. Then cut off the stakes (stems) at the top of the birdcage so that they are even all around. Grasp the reed holding the hang-loop, and push the ends of the reed down through the center of the stakes to the last row of "over and under" weaving on the cage. Secure the ends of the reed with a twist through the weaving, and turn them back up alongside the stakes.

14. Bind off the ends of the stakes at the top of the birdcage by winding a few wet stems or reed tightly around them. After the stakes have been securely bound, push the ends of the stems (or reed) down into the center of the stakes to hide and secure them.

Making the Birdcage Door

15. The door has a 4" x 4" opening across four of the stakes. The hinge will be at one stake and the latch at another. Begin making the door by laying five 4"-long stem pieces parallel, 1/2" apart.

16. Bend a reed in half to use as a weaver, and begin at the center to twine across the pieces. Continue twining back and forth until you have finished the bottom half of the door.

17. Take another weaver and do the same across the upper half. The door will get firmer as you complete the weaving.

18. Make loops for a door hinge on one side of the door. The loops should be slightly open so that you can slip one straight, 6" piece of reed through these loops to attach the door to one stem of the cage.

19. Clip off the three stems in the doorway. The top of the doorway is just under the center of the cage below the upsett, and the bottom is at the two rows of twining between the center and the base.

20. A door latch can be constructed from a strip of braided raffia.

Bottom of the Cage

21. Set the cage on a piece of paper, and draw a circle approximately the same size as the interior circumference of the base of your cage.

22. Use this pattern to draw and cut a base from heavier posterboard. Then cut several new cattail stems to fit next to one another, covering the top surface of the base. Glue these in place.

23. Cut four stems long enough to use above and below the base as supporters. (Refer to the illustration and photo.) When the glue is dry, slip the base (with the attached stems facing up) into position in the cage. Place two supporter stems underneath the base and two on top of the base. Rest the supporters on the rows of twining at the base of the cage.

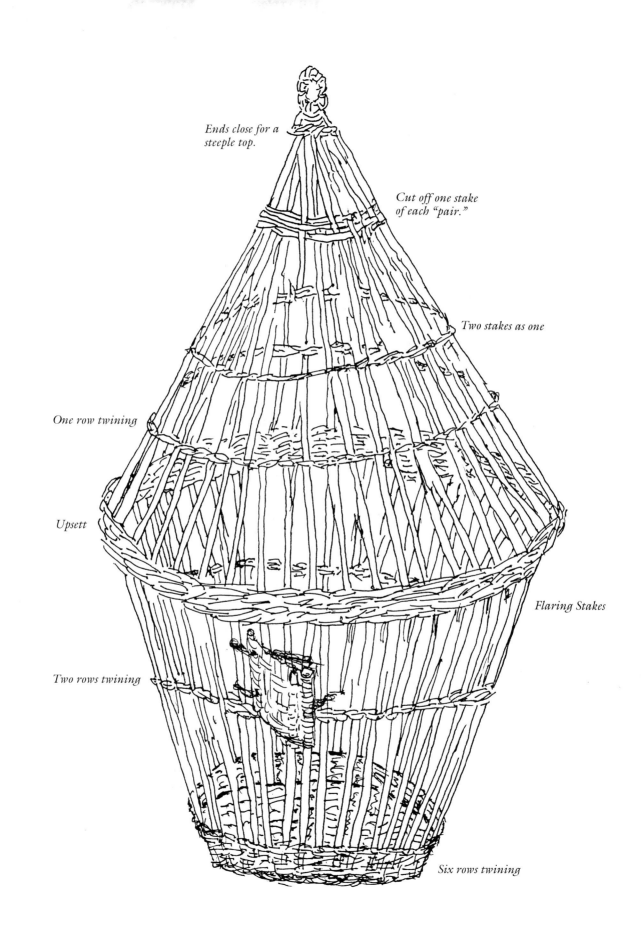

Ends close for a
steeple top.

Cut off one stake
of each "pair."

Two stakes as one

One row twining

Upsett

Flaring Stakes

Two rows twining

Six rows twining

Vine Wallflower Basket

see photo page 73

To make an enchanting basket that you can hang on your wall, all you need is an armful of vines. Vines are so easy to find, usually free for the asking, and most often grow in places where they need to be cut back. Wrapped and laced into this oval shape, the vines make a versatile base to show off plants and flowers at the front porch or on the deck.

One of the best times of the year to cut vines and pull the runners is September through October. You'll find them growing on the ground, in bushes, even climbing trees.

The rustic charm of this pocket basket comes from the rough, reddish texture of honeysuckle bark. Many other vines work equally well; wisteria, woodvine, and grapevine are a few examples.

MATERIALS

    35-40 lengths of thin, flexible vine
    garden gloves or two cloth towels
    raffia strips (optional)
    moss
    potting soil
    flowering plants

TOOLS

    scissors
    measuring tape or yardstick

INSTRUCTIONS

1. Strip off any leaves and unwanted branches by holding the vine at the top end and gently pulling the whole length of vine through your hand (protected by a glove or cloth)

2. Coil all of the lengths of stripped vines together, and let them soak in a sink or tub of water for half an hour

Making the Oval Base

3. Count 10 to 15 vine strips, pull them from the water, and lay them in front of you.

4. Estimate the center of the bunch to establish the bottom midpoint of the oval. Slide your hands apart along the vines, moving outward from the center, and bend the two sides of the bunch toward each other so that they create an oval shape.

5. Cross one set of ends over the other. Now loop one side over and up through the inside of the oval. Repeat this looping (wrapping) with the other vine ends, making long spirals around the oval.

If your vines are rather stiff, you will only be able to pull through the circle a couple of times. With smaller, more bendable vines, you can wrap much closer together, and you will see the spiral pattern. Secure the ends by tucking them into the center of the oval base.

Making the Plant Holder Cross Strip

6. Taking about 15 vines together, lay the bunch lengthwise across the center of the oval. Bend this group of vines outward to form the middle edge of the plant holder part of the basket. (See the illustration on the next page.)

7. Loop the ends of the vines around the outside of the oval, and wrap the ends from both sides back toward the center. Secure the ends by tucking them into the vines.

8. Now take a single, long vine, and wrap it in a figure-eight motion around the middle group of vines. Start at one end where the middle group of vines attaches to the oval base. Continue to spiral wrap all the way across, ending with a figure-eight wrap securing the middle group to the opposite end of the oval base. Repeat the wrapping, going across in the opposite direction for more firmness to the middle group of vines.

Lacing the Base and Pocket

9. Next, using your longest, and strongest vine strips, secure one end into the top, far right corner of the oval base. Lace the vine from the top of the base down to the bottom, and up into the pocket bundle. Then lace the vine back down to the bottom of the pocket, and up to the top of oval base.

10. Using another long vine, lace across the oval base and plant pocket. Complete the lacing with a total of approximately 15 rows across and 15 down.

11. If you feel that the pocket needs added strength, lash raffia at the joints where the oval base and middle pocket vine bundles meet.

12. Line the vine pocket with moss, and fill it with dirt and flowering plants.

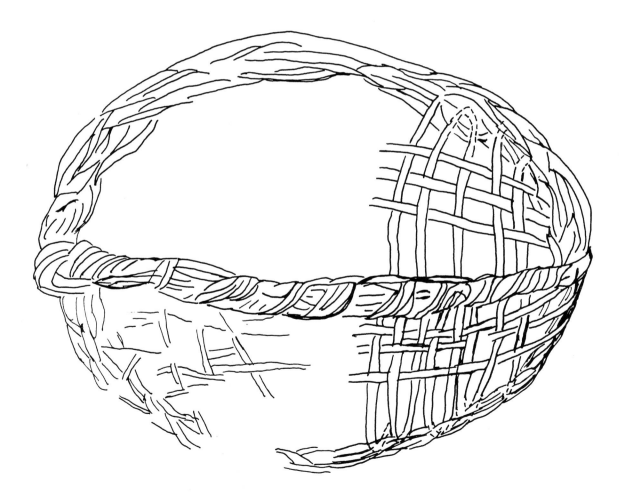

Ornamental Goose "Decoy"

see photo page 72

America's art of decoy-making began over a thousand years ago with Native American lures made from woven reeds and stuffed bird skins. Children were entertained with toy floating "ducks" made by banding coiled cattail leaves together. The American colonists whittled goose decoys from wood.

This goose comes direct from the marshlands where cattails and water-loving grasses grow. It is made from cattails gathered in late fall when the stalks and leaves are dried and the color is a satiny buff-beige.

Look for long, solid stems with sword-like leaves at the base. Grasp the side leaves along with the stalk, and cut them all together at the base with a sharp knife. You will need about 30 stalks to make this life-size goose.

MATERIALS

    30 cattail stalks
    rubber bands
    #3 braided picture wire
    (1) 7" aluminum nail (eaves trough nail)
    balsa wood block, 2" x 2" x 10"
    black and white paint (optional)
    2" grosgrain ribbon
    cluster of berries (pepper berries or larger)

TOOLS

    utility or craft knife
    pliers
    straight pins
    glue gun
    sandpaper, heavy and medium
    scissors or hacksaw

INSTRUCTIONS

1. Begin by selecting your best stalks, those which are straight and undamaged. Cut 20" pieces from the best-looking part of the round, firm stalks. Slice the 20" sections lengthwise into 1/4"-wide strips. You will probably get two to four strips per stalk.

2. When you have enough to make a bunch about 20" in circumference, compress them into a compact bundle. Form the bundle into an oval shape that is slightly flattened on top and bottom.

3. Use rubber bands to hold your body-bundle together, and wrap it firmly with heavy picture wire. Wrap one 26" piece of wire around the body bundle about 4" from the front, and the other wire 7" from the first (see Figure 1). Finish wrapping with the ends of the wire on the bottom of the bundle. Pull and twist the wire ends with pliers to secure them firmly.

Braided picture wire is twisted firmly around body-bundle.

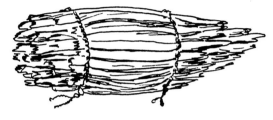

Figure 1

4. Now, with the wires twisted tightly enough to keep the body bundle very firm, you are ready to shape your goose decoy. Begin by cutting away the excess portions at the breast and tail sections (here a hacksaw works very well, or good, sharp scissors). Cut away from the underside of the back (tail) area in a slope from the belly up to the tip of the tail (see Figure 1). Cut a somewhat sloping "V" into the front section. This will be rounded off smoothly to give form to the breast. After the basic shaping you are ready for the final shaping of the breast and tail.

5. Using a utility knife, or comparable cutting tool, whittle, shave, and slice to achieve a desirable breast and tail shape to the body bundle. When the body is pretty well shaped, use a heavy sandpaper to smooth over the reed ends. The sandpaper finish will give a somewhat feathery look to the ends of the cattail pieces.

6. Now you are ready to add body padding to shape the rounded mid-section of the goose. You are padding the center to form contours that will be covered with 7" smooth cattail strips placed parallel to each other around the body bundle between the wires.

Begin this shaping by cutting two long, smooth cattail strips 3/4" to 1" wide. Beginning at the center section behind the first wire, attach one end of the strip using a straight pin, and begin to wind the strip around the body section. Finish wrapping one strip around, pin it in place, and begin with another. Pin each strip into place as you round out the mid-section between the wires.

7. Next cut 25 to 30 strips 7" long from the smoothest cattails. Untwist the wire bands so that they are slightly less than tight (your rubber bands can still be in place to hold the body-bundle strips in place). Begin to lay the 7" strips lengthwise around the body bundle. Slip the ends of the 7" strips just under the rubber bands (or wires), allowing them to protrude about a 1/2" beyond the wires or rubber bands. With all of the 7" pieces in place, completely covering the padding strips, you are ready to again firmly twist and pull the wires as before. Blend the ends of the 7" pieces into the body-bundle by gently shaving the tips and sanding them.

8. Cover the wires using two long, smooth 1"-wide cattail strips. Wrap the strips around and pin them (with straight pins) in place on the bottom side. Applying glue to these strips helps hold them in place over the wires.

9. The goose head is roughed out of a balsa wood block measuring 2" x 2" x 10". Cut the block to 7" long, and glue the cut 3" piece to the side of the 7" block to form the beak of the goose head. Using the pattern in Figure 2, sketch a side view of the head (top, bill and neck) onto the balsa block. Cut and shape the head with your knife and heavy sandpaper (sandpaper does the job very well and is easy to work with). Finish with a medium weight sandpaper.

10. Use one 7" aluminum nail to drive up through the bottom of the body bundle so that it protrudes at the top in front of the wire. Twist the balsa head into place onto the tip of the nail. Use glue on the neck portion to help secure the head onto the body. (See Figure 3.)

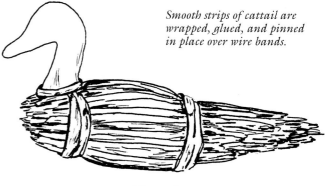

Smooth strips of cattail are wrapped, glued, and pinned in place over wire bands.

Figure 3

11. You can either paint the head of your goose or leave it natural. Tie the ribbon around the neck at the neck-body joint. Insert the berry cluster for added decoration.

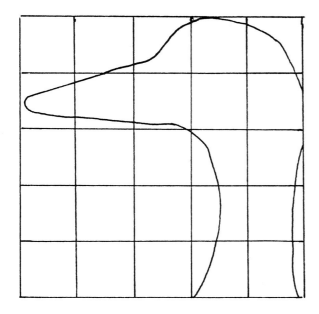

To Scale: 1 square = 1"

Figure 2

One Leaf At A Time

see photo page 72

In "Hushed October," poet Robert Frost wrote of autumn: "Beguile us in the way you know, release one leaf at break of day:…Enchant the land with amethyst." And so we wander, picking up one leaf at a time, to press, to sort by color, and recreate a fantasy of falling leaves of our own in the hush of October.

Using freshly fallen, brightly colored leaves the way some artists use paint, we can create a leaf painting. We can arrange the leaves by color, by size, and we can use the leaf stems for dimension.

MATERIALS

leaves: green, yellow, red, orange
(the arrangement works best using
leaves from one tree)
plexiglass, 12" x 18"
clear-drying Tacky Glue (available
at craft stores)
Glass Kote (a craft finish)
ready-made frame, 12" x 18"

TOOLS

leaf press
2" flat brush

INSTRUCTIONS

1. Find a tree with freshly dropped leaves, and pick up variety of colors and sizes (to be sorted later).

2. Press the leaves (with the stems attached) in a leaf press for four days.

3. Remove the leaves from the press, and sort them. If you spread them out on a light background, it is easier to distinguish different shades of color and to arrange the leaves.

4. Group the leaves by color, and lay them out to determine their sizes, ranging from large to tiny.

5. Determine your leaf arrangement by laying the leaves out in a design you like, saving the best leaves to use across the top.

6. Begin gluing the leaves to the plexiglass, starting at the top and going from left to right, overlapping the leaves as you go. Use a watered-down solution of the Tacky Glue, and apply it with the brush.

7. Install the ready-made frame following the manufacturer's directions. The "frameless" look of the painting in the photo (page 72) was achieved using a Uni-Frame, an expandable mounting system that only reveals a pair of clips on each edge of the painting.

An optional mounting technique is to drill two small holes at the top edge of the plexiglass before you attach the leaves. After the leaves have been glued in place, tie two double strands of raffia through the holes. Place the knots on the reverse side, and make a simple, natural hanger with the raffia.

Hydrangea and Sweet Annie Heart Wreaths

see photos page 71

Hydrangea blossoms that beg to be picked, are turning to the softest shades of pink, peach, and green in the fall. Beautifully shaped to follow the heart form of grapevines, they make a delicate reminder of love.

Dried Sweet Annie—so often found on the woodland trails among the wild grasses—here follows the heart shape of wisteria vines. You can discover your own Sweet Annie as you hike through the woodlands, or you can buy it by the bundle from a plant center that sells dried flowers.

MATERIALS

> 6–8 lengths of vine, each 60" long, for each
> wreath: grapevine or #4 reed for
> hydrangea wreath; wisteria or #2 reed
> for Sweet Annie wreath
> hydrangea blossoms or Sweet Annie
> dried roses
> 12" square board
> 3" nails

TOOLS

> hammer
> glue gun

INSTRUCTIONS

Grapevines are the easiest vines to use for making a wreath, large or small, and they are usually free for the asking. Grapevine heart wreaths can also be found in your local plant centers. Another option is wisteria vine, which is boiled, stripped of its bark, then cut into approximately six to eight 60" lengths. Alternatively, you can purchase #4 reed, cut it into the needed lengths, and soak it in water.

Making a Heart-Shaped Wreath

1. First choose which wreath you want to make, and select your vine or reed accordingly. Lay several damp lengths of vine or reed together. Using both hands, bend the bundle at the center (the heart's point). Shape the sides of the heart; then curve the ends down at the top center, pointing them inward to make a heart shape. Wire the ends together firmly. Attach one 4" hanger wire at the back for hanging later. Notice that the shape is more round than heartlike at this point.

2. Hammer three 3" nails into the 12" board in an upside down triangle pattern (two at the top and one at the bottom point) so that they will fit inside the wreath. Lay the wreath on the board around the nails. You can add more nails if necessary to hold the vines firmly in a heart shape until the wreath is dry.

Decorating Your Wreath

3. For the hydrangea wreath, begin gluing dried blossoms along the front of the wreath, choosing blossoms that best fit the heart shape. Fill in the outer and inner edges with small flowers trimmed to shape. Cut some blossoms in half, and glue the flat side to the wreath. Keep the heart shape as obvious as possible. Glue about five smaller blossoms (dried yellow or red tea roses) in places that enhance the heart shape.

4. Use a sheer, wire-edge ribbon in peach or another light color to finish your hydrangea wreath. Tie a wide, cross-over knot at the center of an 18" length of ribbon, and gently glue the knot at the top center "point" of the wreath. Bend the ribbon to flow outward and down, making your own ribbon design. Glue it into place.

5. For the more delicate, Sweet Annie wreath, glue the blossoms all around your heart-shaped wreath. Glue a large dried rose at the top center of the heart, on top of the Sweet Annie. Add smaller flower decorations to the sides of the heart.

Cattail Toy Chair

see photo page 77

Did you know that many of the cattails that you see growing along the roadside also cover miles of swamp and marshlands throughout the world? Not only are they ornamental, but they're practical too. The roots are rich in starch and can actually be eaten like a potato; the fluff (or down) has been used in life jackets, baseballs, and mattresses. In Europe the fluff is used for tinder. The leaves are used to make baskets and rush seats for chairs.

When you see the cattail without its thick, brown top you see a slender, sturdy stem four to six feet long. This is called cattail "timber."

Toy chairs—ladder back or rocker—that are made from the stems (the cattail timber) are easy and fun to make. With a little help on the measuring and cutting, even a six-year-old child can make this miniature furniture.

MATERIALS

> several cattail stems
> straight pins
> raffia, moistened (for a woven seat)
> lightweight cardboard and paint (alternative
>   seat design)
> small length of splint (for a rocker)

TOOLS

> scissors

INSTRUCTIONS

Making the Chair Frame

1. Cut the following pieces from small or middle sections of the cattail stems:

> 2 back legs, each 5"
>
> 2 front legs, each 2"
>
> 6 ladder rungs, each 1-1/2"
>
> 4 side rungs, each 1-1/2"

2. Place the two 5" pieces parallel to each other, and accurately mark off the pin hole positions as noted in the illustration.

3. Join the two 5" back pieces with four of the six ladder rungs as shown in the illustration. Position and secure the rungs with straight pins, pushing the pins through the marked pin holes.

4. Take the two front legs and follow the same procedure as above, fastening the remaining two ladder rungs in place.

5. Mark the pin holes for joining the front legs with the back using the 1-1/2" side rungs, two to each side (follow the illustration).

6. At this point, level the chair and make any adjustments necessary for it to stand straight and firm. Then, to strengthen it, glue each of the joints, and let them dry. (Gluing the joints after the piece is together makes a straighter and stronger chair than gluing each joint as it is assembled.)

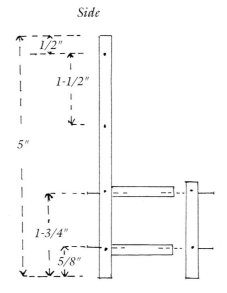

Side

1/2"

1-1/2"

5"

1-3/4"

5/8"

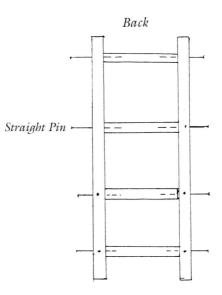

Back

Straight Pin

Woven Chair Seat

Thread a yarn needle with a long piece of raffia, and tie the free end to the back corner of the chair seat. Twist the raffia into a cord and start working from the back to the front over and under the seat rungs until the cord crosses about ten times. Then bring the raffia under the front corner and out to the side. Now start weaving across the top of the seat to the other side. To come back to the first side, pass the raffia under the seat without weaving it in, and continue until the seat is woven. Finish at the same corner where the raffia was tied to start. Tie the two ends of the raffia together, cut, and tuck them under. Shellac or varnish the chair.

Corrugated Cardboard Seat

Trace the seat pattern onto a piece of light corrugated cardboard; cut, and paint the seat your choice of color and design. Then glue the seat into place.

Rocking Chair

After finishing the chair and seat, you can make the rocker pieces by cutting and shaping them from a strip of splint. Then pin and glue the rockers in place.

Candy "Keepsake" Basket

see photo page 76

This little basket, made with the simplest of weaves, is most intriguing when made with a combination of the lighter, peeled honeysuckle vines and darker, unpeeled vines. Charming for many purposes—even as guest soap baskets—these little vine baskets make delightful keepsake candy baskets.

MATERIALS

   1 heavier vine (the "weaver")
   8 long vines, all the same length (for "stakes")

TOOLS

   scissors or clippers

INSTRUCTIONS

1. Pinch and bend the "weaver" vine at its center, and set it aside.

2. Separate the eight vines into four pairs (these are the "stakes"). These stakes will be used in pairs to give the basket extra sturdiness.

3. Arrange the four pairs of vines like spokes in a wheel.

4. Hold the spokes at the center point with one hand. With the other hand, slip the center bend of the weaver vine around the bottom pair of stakes so that both ends of the weaver are pointing in the same direction.

5. Weave these ends around the stakes so that while one length of the weaver goes over a pair of stakes, the other length goes under the same pair.

6. As you run out of weaver length, you will need to introduce a new weaver. Just loop in the new weaver next to the one being ended, and proceed around the basket.

7. Continue weaving until the sides are as high as you want, keeping the weave as tight as possible.

8. Finish the basket by directing the stakes of each pair past the adjacent pair, and bending them into the weave itself. Push them down and through, and clip off the excess.

Festive Autumn Peppers Laced on a Raffia Rope

see photo page 74

This colorful array of red hot peppers instantly becomes a bright and beautiful part of your kitchen decor when sewn to a swag of raffia rope. These long, skinny peppers, which are sometimes used in fruit, floral, and wreath arrangements, are really quite unusual. They keep their bright, pretty color even while drying, and you can spray the peppers with a clear acrylic gloss to preserve them.

The pungent, pod-like fruit can be found in any of several varieties in the food store or drying by the bundle in the marketplace. If you like to garden, you'll enjoy growing your own assortment of the smaller, ornamental peppers. You'll find that their brilliant colors, smooth and shiny surface, and fascinating shapes make interesting arrangements like this "pepper rope" for the kitchen. Fiery hot peppers like the long red cayenne, Hungarian wax, or Anaheim can be used in cooking too!

MATERIALS

    1 bundle of raffia
    assortment of 25-30 hot peppers

TOOLS

    yarn needle
    scissors

INSTRUCTIONS

The Raffia Braid

1. The rope used for this project was purchased in a craft store, but it is very easy to make your own double-braided rope. Pull out 25 to 30 strands of raffia, and cut them 24" long. Wrap and tie one piece of raffia around the bundle 5" from the top. Divide the strands into three bunches, and braid the raffia.

2. Make a loop with the braid by tying the two ends together at the bottom. The top few inches of the loop is used as a hanger, and the rest of the braid is covered with another layer of braided raffia.

3. Insert the rest of the raffia through this braided loop and secure it firmly in place with a length of raffia, leaving the top few inches of the braided loop free to serve as a hanger. Divide the loose raffia into three large bundles and braid them over the full length of the first braid. The completed double-braided rope should be approximately 36" long. Tie off the braid about 8" from the bottom ends.

4. Choose the best 25 or 30 peppers, and lay them alongside your braided rope. The peppers don't need to be dried beforehand because they will dry as they hang on the rope. Arrange them by color, shape, and size to get the combination you like best. The peppers should hang a little off-set from each other, not directly over one other. Leave an inch or so between each pepper.

5. Thread your yarn needle with a thin strip of raffia. With the braided raffia rope and pepper arrangement all ready, begin sewing the peppers in place. Knot the raffia strip at the back of the braided rope, bring the needle to the front, and slip the needle through the back of your first pepper. After securing the pepper in place, push the needle back down through the raffia rope. Continue sewing the peppers one by one onto the rope until the arrangement is complete.

6. Hang your arrangement of autumn peppers and raffia braid in the kitchen as a decoration.

Pepper Berry Wreath Mirror
see photo page 75

Discovering pepper-berry branches on a woodland trail of wild field grasses can be the inspiration for making your own wreath mirror with one of nature's prettiest, most colorful shrubs.

Design your own mirror frame with a fascinating arrangement of moss and colorful, dried berry bush sprigs. Surprisingly, this natural composition can provide a kind of restorative power that comes to us from the great outdoors or country garden. This wreath mirror is 13" in diameter, fun and easy to make, and a real treat for all to enjoy!

MATERIALS

mirror, single thickness, 10"-diameter circle
2 pieces of strong corrugated cardboard,
    each a 13"-diameter circle
duct tape
1/4" x 2" wood strip 13" long
glue
picture wire
moss
dried berry branches (pepper berry or
    Sweet Annie)

TOOLS

pencil
ruler
sharp knife
glue gun
staple gun

INSTRUCTIONS

1. Measure and cut two cardboard circles 13" in diameter (a 13" plate serves as good pattern). Cut the two together, or use the first as a pattern for the second so that the two circles are identical to each other.

2. Cut a 9" diameter circle out of the center of one cardboard circle. The resulting frame will measure 2" wide.

.3. Center the mirror onto the back (uncut) cardboard piece, and tape it in place. Use four pieces of duct tape, each about 2" long, being careful not to let the tape overlap too much so that it shows on the mirror.

4. Glue the front cardboard frame to the back cardboard circle, and secure it firmly in place. Allow adequate drying time.

5. Glue the wood strip across the middle of the cardboard back. Let the glue dry thoroughly.

6. Attach a picture hanging wire to the wood piece using heavy duty staples. Be careful not to apply any staples into the back of the glass mirror.

7. Glue moss carefully around the entire front frame, pressing the moss firmly and carefully into place.

8. Glue the dried sprigs of berries onto the moss using your own imagination and design. Wildflowers and herbs can be added to complement the berries.

Five Little Pumpkins
All in a Row
see photo page 74

A bountiful harvest in the pumpkin fields means that it is time for the change of seasons, and time to gather pumpkins in all sizes.

An arrangement of pumpkins symbolizes autumn, and jack-o-lanterns with grinning faces have been part of the Halloween festivities for generations. Face lines are drawn on the pumpkins, then cut out, and a candle put inside to bring the faces to life.

These five little Halloween pumpkins, each with different face lines, are not cut, but are wired on a braid of raffia rope to greet "trick-or-treaters" that come to your door.

MATERIALS

    1 bundle of raffia
    5 miniature pumpkins with stems
    black marking pen
    10 pieces of #22 gauge wire

TOOLS

    awl
    wire cutters

INSTRUCTIONS

Make a Raffia Braid

    1. Gather 25 to 30 strands of raffia into a bundle, and cut the strands 24" long. Wrap and tie one piece of raffia around the bundle 5" from the top. Divide the strands into three bunches, and braid the raffia. Finish by bringing the end of the braid back to the beginning point and tying the ends together.

    2. Hold the braid so that the midpoint of the loop is at the top and the tied ends are at the bottom. Grasp the two sides of the braid and hold them together. The top 2" to 3" of the loop will serve as a hanger, and the balance will be used as a core to "fatten up" the finished braid.

    3. Insert the rest of the raffia through this braided loop, leaving the top few inches of the loop free to use as a hanger. Using one piece of

Back of Pumpkin

Front of Pumpkin

raffia, tie the bundle to the braid (refer to the photograph).

4. Divide the bundle into three components, and braid over the complete length of the existing braid. The finished raffia rope should be approximately 36" long. Tie off the braid about 8" from the bottom ends.

Hanging the Pumpkins

5. Pierce two holes on each side of, and a little behind, the stem on each pumpkin. The holes should go through the pumpkin from top to bottom (see the illustration).

6. Insert one length of wire into each hole, leaving an equivalent amount of wire outside each top and bottom hole. Twist the two top wires together with five or six twists, and do the same with the bottom wires.

7. Starting at the top of the raffia braid, attach a pumpkin by pushing the wires through the raffia from the front side to the back, first the top wires then the bottom wires. (The easiest way to pierce the raffia is to push through one set of wire ends at a time.)

8. Secure the pumpkin in place by twisting the two top wires with the two bottom wires. Make six to eight twists (into one twist), cut the wires, and bend the ends back into the raffia.

9. Secure the remaining four pumpkins the same way.

10. Hang up the raffia braid with its attached pumpkins so that you can determine where you want to make the face designs on each pumpkin. Draw the face designs with a black marking pen. Then take down the pumpkin braid, and retouch the lines with the black pen.

Paper Ribbon Party Pumpkins

see photo page 76

Real or unreal, pumpkins are fun to shape with a knife or with just a few yards of stretchy paper ribbon, string, and glue!

Consider having a real pumpkin carving party for the kids, and a paper pumpkin making party for the grown-ups, with a competition for both. To make a paper pumpkin, just cut, twist, and tie the ribbon. Then gently glue the shape together. It's a pumpkin to fool the eye!

MATERIALS (for one paper pumpkin)

    4 yards of 2"-wide paper ribbon in pumpkin or natural color

    cotton string

    glue

TOOLS

    scissors

    glue gun

INSTRUCTIONS

Note: These directions are for making one paper pumpkin approximately 8" in diameter. Each pumpkin is made of four sections. Adjust the size of your pumpkins by increasing or decreasing the number and length of the ribbon sections.

1. Uncoil the paper ribbon, and cut four 36" lengths.

2. Begin by holding one 36" piece of ribbon in your hand with the end extending about 3" above your hand. These 3"-long ends are twisted and glued together to make the stem after all four sections have been put together.

3. Bring the ribbon down and out from the bottom of your hand, and begin wrapping the ribbon loosely around your hand from front to back, overlapping four times.

4. Pinch the center, inside wraps of the ribbon together, and tie them firmly with string. Set this first section aside, and repeat the process with three additional sections.

5. Shape your pumpkin sections by spreading the ribbon and placing the most complementary sections next to one another.

6. Tie three of the ribbon sections together at their centers, shape again, and finally add the last section to the first.

7. Check the overlapping edges of the ribbon around the entire pumpkin, and glue any ribbon edges where needed,

8. Open the stem ends of the ribbon, put the flat ends together, then twist all of these together to make one stem. Use glue if needed.

Golden Gourd Ribbon Box

see photo page 77

Gourds have been used for centuries as food and water containers. Hard shell gourds that have been found in Egyptian tombs date back to 2400 B.C. In Mexico, gourds were used for bottles as early as 7000 B.C. American pioneers used this "cousin to the pumpkin and squash" as a bowl and dipper, and for a baby rattle.

Gourds, because of their remarkable color patterns and shapes, are probably the most unusual plants in the garden. The variety used for this ribbon box is a single color, pear-shaped gourd.

Search the markets, if you don't have a garden nearby, for pear-shaped gourds that are 6-8" high. Look for those with a smooth skin, except for a few dabbles of bumps, to make a box with an intriguing texture to cut and paint.

MATERIALS

ornamental gourd (with prominent neck),
    cured and cleaned
gold acrylic or metallic paint
lacquer (optional)

TOOLS

pencil or fine point marking pen
craft knife, sharp knife or fine-toothed hack
    saw
spoon

INSTRUCTIONS

1. Find a pear-shaped ornamental gourd that has been allowed to cure in the field, making it hard but light in weight.

2. Hammer a small nail into the top, near the stem, and make a similar hole in the bottom.

3. Just below the prominent neck, where the gourd begins to slope outward, mark a cutting line that will indicate the top "lid" and bottom "box" pieces.

4. Cut off the top with a knife or a fine-toothed hacksaw.

5. To remove the soft pulp from inside the gourd, soak the top and bottom pieces in soapy water, and scrape them out with a spoon. The inside will feel firm and smooth.

6. Allow the shell to dry in an airy, shady place for about ten days. While it is drying, turn the gourd every day, and wipe off any moisture that has condensed on the shell. Press the edges of the "lid" firmly between your fingers each day of drying (this keeps the edges from curling inward). Make sure that the gourd has become hard and light in weight before painting it.

7. Paint the entire gourd, inside and out, with gold acrylic paint. Let it dry.

8. As an optional step, coat the painted gourd with lacquer.

Apple "Star" Wreath

see photo page 78

Apples and fall just seem to go together. This is the time of year to go to the orchard and pick your own, climbing high up into the trees, or for the less daring, to stand on the ground and choose the best juicy apples from the lower branches. If you don't want to pick them, they are bountiful at roadside stands and at the grocery store. It's fun to come home with a bagful to munch on, saving some for a yummy apple pie, and of course, some for crafting!

With this dried apple wreath, you can enjoy those wonderful fall apples all year round. It's a perfect accent for your kitchen wall or a door. All you need are six apples, all approximately the same size. The slices are easy to soak and dry, and the seed holes leave a natural star design in the center.

MATERIALS

6 large, unblemished apples
salt
lemon
1 yard 1/8" red satin ribbon
1 yard paper twist, natural
plastic fruit cluster
2 metal rings, 8" and 9"
thick craft glue
clear acrylic finish, small jar
masking tape
paper towels

TOOLS

sharp knife
paintbrush, #4 or #6
shallow bowl
wire rack or broiler pan
oven
tape measure
scissors

INSTRUCTIONS

1. Slice each apple horizontally into 1/8" slices. The core of each center slice will have a star design. To make one wreath, choose approximately 20 center slices with well defined star designs.

2. Squeeze the juice from a lemon into the bowl. Add one teaspoon of salt, and stir well. Soak the apple slices for two to three minutes in the juice, covering them completely, and turning the slices once. Remove the apple slices one at a time, and place them in a single layer on the paper towels. Pat the slices with a paper towel to absorb excess moisture.

3. Place the slices on the wire screen or broiler pan, and place them into a warm oven (about 150°) for four to six hours. Remove the slices from the oven and let them cool. (The cooled apple slices may be stored in an air-tight container until needed.)

4. Place the 8" ring inside the 9" ring on a flat surface. Completely wrap the two together with masking tape to form a 1"- wide flat wreath base.

5. Leaving a 2-1/2" opening for the bow, glue the apple slices onto the wreath base, overlapping the edges. After letting the glue dry, brush the apple slices with two coats of acrylic finish. Allow the finish to dry between coats. Afterward, apply finish to the back of the slices.

6. Tie a paper twist into a 6" bow with streamers, notching the ends of the streamers. Tie a satin ribbon into a bow, and glue it to the center of the paper twist bow. Finally, glue a fruit cluster to the bow centers.

*Winter's
chill brings
a quiet
tranquility
and stark
beauty
to the
landscape.*

Aromatic bay leaves take on a whole new sophistication when gilded. Frame a rectangular mirror for the hallway, or create a heart-shaped wreath for the front door. Directions for the mirror are on page 112, and the wreath on page 113.

While leisurely walking through a pine forest, take the time to collect some pine needles. These, together with some raffia, can be woven into handsome baskets that retain a delicious pine aroma. See page 109 for instructions.

Winter is the perfect time to assemble topiaries that can be changed to reflect each season. Start with a tree top covering of pepper berries and tiny cones, and when the season changes, replace the top with one covered in flowers. Directions start on page 106.

99

A rustic lamp crafted from tree branches makes a dramatic accent for most any decor. With pre-assembled lamp parts, the wiring is a breeze and can be done in under an hour. Directions are on page 105.

Raffia tassels make delightful accents, especially when they include gold lamé threads. Use them for trimming gift packages and to complete rice paper sachets filled with fragrant potpourri. The tassels are described on page 115, and the sachets on page 113.

Making natural ornaments for the Christmas tree is fun for the whole family. Start with sand dollars collected at the beach, and add a simple bow with a few berries. See page 118 for directions. For the children, make ice cream cones in "chocolate" (pine cones) and "vanilla" (dried white flowers), and fill glass ball ornaments with scented potpourri. The ice cream ornaments are described on page 121, and the potpourri-filled glass balls on page 120. Weave cattail leaves into tiny reindeer that will leap onto the Christmas tree. Instructions begin on page 116.

Combining a love of basketry with a need for Christmas tree ornaments yields a delicate basket to fill with miniature pine cones or sprigs of berries. Instructions are on page 119.

Birds have special needs in winter, when food can be harder for them to find. A suet feeder hung from a tree provides birds with good nutrition and a compelling reason to visit your backyard. The feeder is simple in construction, and your efforts will be well rewarded with the companionship of feathered friends. See page 108 for directions.

Rustic Table Lamp

see photo page 100

Late 19th century tourists visiting national parks such as Yellowstone and Yosemite were captivated by the rustic chairs, tables, and lamps that furnished the lodges and hotels. These were made by local craftsmen from readily available tree branches.

Again there seems to be a need to bring natural forms of wood back into our everyday lives. Homeowners—even designers—are clamoring for the raw and rustic tables, lamps, and chairs. These become a delightful, everyday reminder of nature.

This rustic table lamp is made from the branches of an alderwood tree. From its base to the top edge of its rice paper lamp shade, the lamp stands approximately 18" tall.

MATERIALS

4 branches of alderwood (or willow, birch, poplar, other), each 10" x 1" diameter
4 branches, each 5" x 1" diameter
(36) 2" coated finishing nails
lamp/switch replacement kit
white paper lamp shade
one sheet of rice paper
tacky glue
paper tape

TOOLS

hammer
drill
"C" clamp
sandpaper

INSTRUCTIONS

Construct the Lamp Base

1. Trim and sand smooth the cut ends of all of the wood pieces.

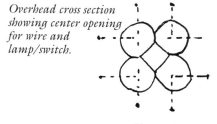

Overhead cross section showing center opening for wire and lamp/switch.

Figure 1

2. Trim FLAT the full length of one side of each of the four 10" branches. When the branches are clustered together, this provides an opening down the center for the wire to travel from the base to the top. (See Figure 1.)

3. Referring to the arrangement shown in Figure 1, nail the four 10" branches together near the top, center, and bottom. Apply a "C" clamp around the two pieces being nailed (if the wood is not perfectly straight, the clamp assures better alignment). Be sure to drill a pilot hole for each nail so that the wood won't split.

4. When all four uprights have been nailed into place, attach the base pieces. Apply one 5" piece horizontally to each side, as shown in Figure 2. Make certain that the lamp stands perfectly straight when resting on the base.

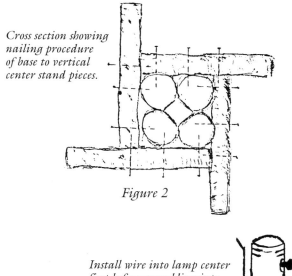

Cross section showing nailing procedure of base to vertical center stand pieces.

Figure 2

Install wire into lamp center first before assembling into lamp/switch kit.

5. Sand the bottom edges of the base pieces to flatten them and provide greater stability.

6. Countersink all of the nails, fill the holes with putty, and wax or polish the surface.

Figure 3

7. Following the manufacturer's instructions, install the lamp/switch kit (see Figure 3). Most lamp/switch replacement kits contain everything needed to finish the construction (except the shade and bulb).

Rice Paper Lamp Shade Covering

8. Draw a pattern for your shade on tissue paper. Lay the shade on the paper, and begin making your pattern by marking a pencil line that follows the bottom edge of the shade as you roll the shade one complete turn.

9. Repeat, making another pattern line that follows the top edge of the shade.

10. Draw another line along both the top and bottom edges, about 1/2" outside your first pattern line. This extra 1/2" allows enough paper for folding a finish edge to the inside of the shade. Cut out the entire pattern.

11. Secure your tissue pattern onto the rice paper by using bits of paper tape in about six places. Then trace the pattern and cut out the rice paper.

12. Using a watered-down tacky glue, begin at the seam to glue the rice paper onto the shade. Smoothing the paper as you turn the shade, glue a few inches at a time, and press the paper to the shade.

13. When the rice paper is glued in place all around the shade, glue the top and bottom edges, and fold them into place.

Seasonal Twig Topiary Trees

see photo page 99

One of the most basic French ornamental shapes is the standard—a term that refers to a plant trained to grow with a single stem and topped with a rounded growth of flowers and greenery. A bit of seasonal elegance, these topiaries have two twig stems permanently set into clay pots, and the "tree tops" are a rounded, natural bouquet that can change with the season.

Standing 10" tall from pot base to top, these topiaries look best in pairs, making twin trees that you can move from mantel to tabletop. The interchangeable tree tops are a pure delight to make, and they can be completed in just a few hours.

MATERIALS

> 2 twig stems, each 8" x 1/2" diameter
> 2 vines (ivy or grapevine), each 12" long
> 2 clay pots, 3" diameter
> plaster of paris
> rigid plastic foam balls, 2-1/2" diameter (two for each season)
> 3–4 tiny scrap pieces of rigid foam
> dried moss
> 1/2 yard of decorator ribbon
> dried flowers: rose buds, straw flowers, globe, larkspur, or other (dry your own or purchase from a supplier)
> other dried greenery: small pine cones, cedar cones, acorns, tiny leaves, cedar branch tips, pepper berry sprigs, or other berries

TOOLS

> old bowl for mixing plaster of paris
> knife or scissors
> glue gun

INSTRUCTIONS

1. Break three or four very small pieces of scrap rigid foam into each pot (the foam pieces will prevent the pots from cracking when they are filled with plaster).

2. Following the manufacturer's directions, mix

enough plaster of paris to fill each pot to 1/4" below the top edge. Insert one twig stem in each pot.

3. Hold the stem in the center until the plaster hardens around the stem. Check to make sure that the stem is straight.

4. Press a rigid foam ball onto the top of each twig stem, applying gentle but firm pressure (the ball is easier to work with while on the stem).

5. Cut the moss into small pieces (use scissors or a sharp knife on a cutting board). Cover the foam ball with glue, then press bits of crumbled moss onto the glue until the entire ball is lightly coated.

6. Glue moss around the base of the stem, covering the entire plaster surface.

7. Starting at the top center of the ball, begin applying decorations by dabbing a bit of glue (with a glue gun) to the base of each flower, leaf, or cone. Press the decorations in place on the ball.

8. Tie a decorative (wire-edged) ribbon, just below the ball.

Suggested Toppings for Winter, Spring, Summer, and Fall:

Winter Top
1. Cover the ball with moss.

2. Cover the moss completely with dry pepper berries (or other colorful berries)

3. Add tiny pine or cedar cones and cedar tips.

4. Finish by gluing one sprig of berries or one pine cone in the moss at the base. Use the wire-edged decorator ribbon to make a bow at the base of the ball. Optionally, wrap a 12"-long vine (tiny ivy or grapevine) around the twig stem. Be sure to soak the vine to make it flexible before wrapping it around the stem.

Spring Top
1. Cover the ball with pink globe flowers. Collect and dry them, or purchase some from a supplier. If you buy packaged globe tops, drop the dried flowers into a bowl of water, and let them soak for 15 minutes or until the petals separate slightly. Drain and pat them dry with a towel. The flowers are ready to use in minutes.

2. Add small green leaves that have been pressed and dried.

3. Save one choice flower and leaf to push into the moss at the base.

Summer Top
1. Cover the ball with moss.

2. Pinch eight to ten tiny wads of Spanish moss and glue them randomly around the ball.

3. Add dried yellow and red rose buds (your own or from supplier).

4. Glue leaves alongside the rose buds, placing the base of the leaf next to the base of the flower (make the leaves point outward and upward).

5. Add four to six small pine sprigs between the moss clumps, roses, and leaves.

6. Attach sprigs of pepper berries or other berries.

7. Tie a ribbon at the base of the ball.

8. Save one rose bud to glue and press into the moss at the base of the pot.

Autumn Top
1. Start with a covering of green moss and bits of Spanish moss.

2. Cover this with small, pressed leaves in a variety of colors.

3. Add acorns, straw flowers, or dried coxcomb in autumn colors.

4. Tie a ribbon at the base of the ball.

5. Finish by gluing one colored leaf or tiny straw flower on the moss at the base of the pot.

Scrappy Suet Birdfeeder

see photo page 104

Part of the fascination of birds is their willingness to come to feeders. Although their numbers change from season to season, you can watch them feed just about anywhere. One of the most exciting places to watch is a suet birdfeeder, where birds fly in to perch and eat in the open. This feeder is very easy to make, and, using very little wood, it can be made from scrap pieces. To attract smaller birds, use 1/4" wire mesh; if you'd rather feed the larger ones, substitute 1/2" mesh.

MATERIALS

1 piece of 2 x 4 pine or other wood, 12" long
1 piece of 1 x 4 pine or other wood, 10" long
1 piece of 3/4 x 1 pine or other wood,
   5-1/2" long
1 piece of 1/4" plywood, 3-1/2" x 7"
2" coated finishing nails
1 piece of 1/4" or 1/2" mesh, 8" x 8-1/2"
1 package of straw (from a craft store)
paper tape
bamboo or cattail pieces
1 screw eye, 1/2" diameter
Note: The actual size of a 2 x 4 is 1-1/2" x
   3-1/2"; a 1 x 4 measures 3/4" x 3-1/2".

TOOLS

staple gun with 1/4" and 1/2" staples
glue gun

INSTRUCTIONS

1. To make the lower front of the feeder (part "A" in the illustration), measure 2" from one end of the 2 x 4, and draw a line across the face (4" side) of the board. Set your saw at a 45° angle, and make a bevel cut outward from the 2" line. The cut piece should measure 2" on the short face and about 3-1/2" on the longer face.

2. The upper front (B) is a piece of 2 x 4 with an overall length of 2-1/2". Because it is difficult to cut the corners off a small piece, remove the corners before cutting the piece to length. The angle of the cuts is not critical, but be sure to leave at least 1" flat at the center to accommodate the roof ridge (D). Refer to the figure for the dimensions of your cuts.

4. Cut one 10"-long piece of 1 x 4 to make the back wall (C) for the feeder.

5. Saw the top corners on "C" (back wall) to match those on "B" (upper front). Then nail "B" to "C" from the back.

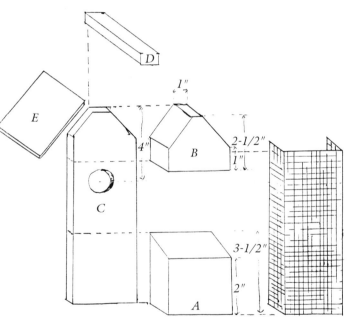

6. Nail "A" (lower front) to "C" from the back. Be careful not to expose any nails through the beveled section of "A." Align the ends for a perfect match.

7. Drill a 1-1/2"-diameter hole centered 4" down from the top end of "C" (refer to the illustration).

8. To make the roof ridge (D), cut one piece of 3/4" x 1" pine 5-1/2" long. Nail the roof ridge to the top end of the birdfeeder, allowing a 2" overhang in front and less in the back.

9. Cut two pieces of 1/4" plywood, each 3-1/2" square for the roof sections (E). Do not attach these until after staining all of the pieces and attaching the wire mesh.

10. Stain the entire birdfeeder with a biodegradable walnut stain before attaching the wire mesh. Let the parts dry completely.

11. Cut a piece of wire mesh 8" x 8-1/2". Fit the mesh around the feeder; then staple it in place with 1/4" staples. Avoid any unnecessary bends in the wire mesh.

12. Attach the roof pieces (E) with 1/2" staples or wire brads. Make sure that the overhang is all at the front and that the roof is flush at the back.

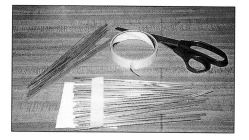

Straw Roof

13. Cut a piece of paper 3-1/2" x 4-1/2".

14. Cut approximately 30 pieces of straw, each about 4-1/2" long.

15. Lay the straw pieces side by side, covering the paper. Press a piece of paper tape across the center of the straw pieces.

16. Spread glue onto one roof side, lift the taped straw pieces as a single group, and press the straw onto the roof. Trim the bottom edges to approximate a 1" overhang. Repeat the process with another layer of straw. Similarly, glue two layers of straw onto the other side of the roof.

17. Cut two strips of bamboo, or cattail stems, each 3-1/2" long. Glue them across the roof straw, pressing them firmly into place.

18. To finish the feeder, attach a screw eye onto the flat center roof ridge, slightly to the rear of the feeder (off balance). When the birdfeeder is filled with suet, the feeder will hang vertically.

Pine Needle Cup Baskets
see photo page 98

You may need to step no further than your own backyard to find the material for making these unique baskets. The basket coils are actually pine needles sewn into various shapes with strands of raffia. Their natural beauty is endearing and easily fits today's decorating trends. Their fresh, almost magical fragrance is an added attraction and a quiet remembrance of the woods.

These baskets are easy to make, and by mastering just a few simple steps, you can produce a number of fascinating shapes and designs. The pine needle cup basket with a lid can be made in just a weekend. Whether it is filled with potpourri or holds fragrant soaps in a guest bath, this basket makes a keepsake piece for holiday time.

From a bundle of damp pine needles, four needles at a time are coiled and sewn with raffia strips into a small basket. The lid is attached with a "hinge" onto the top edge of the basket, and a small pine cone "knob" is sewn on the top center.

The baskets shown here were made with 6–8" needles that can be found and gathered in any wooded area where there are pines. The needles will have to be "cured" if they are not already weathered. Green ones should be laid on a perforated surface until they are dry. You want to dry them to the point where no further shrinkage will occur after the basket is made.

You can leave the needles out in the wind and sun, frost and rain, and they will change to a rich, golden brown. A very good method for curing is to place the needles between two screens that have been tied together (to keep them from being blown away by the wind). Even with this method, you'll need to turn the screens occasionally so that the needles brown evenly on all sides.

When all of the needles have turned an even, golden brown, pull them from the branches and dip them into boiling water to kill any eggs that might later hatch and cause damage. Dry them between layers of a towel. The terry cloth not only dries the needles, but polishes them as well.

Tie the needles in small bundles, keeping the ends all pointed in the same direction. They should be stored in a plastic bag or other container where they lay straight.

Before you use the needles for making a basket, be sure to check them for flexibility. If they're brittle, soak the bundles in clear water for about an hour, or until their resiliency is restored. To keep them pliable while you work, they can be wrapped in damp paper towels, placed in a plastic bag, and kept in your refrigerator.

MATERIALS

> pine needles
> raffia, natural color, long strands
> metal ring, 1" or 2" diameter
> denatured alcohol (optional)
> white shellac (optional)

TOOLS

> yarn needle, #3, #4, #5, #6, or #7
> scissors, embroidery type
> paintbrush (optional)

INSTRUCTIONS

1. To begin the basket, fold one long strand of raffia in half and push the folded end through the center of the ring as shown in Figure 1. Bring the ends of the strand through the "loop" made by the fold and pull the "knot" taut to the outer edge of the ring as shown in Figure 2.

Figure 1   *Figure 2*

2. Bring one raffia end over the front of the ring and down. The other raffia end is left in its original position. The two raffia ends should always be separated in this manner, and it is important that the upper strand remain in place when not making a stitch.

3. Hold the ring in your left hand; you will be working from left to right. Take the upper raffia strand by its end, bring it through the ring from the back and through the loop it forms, as shown in Figure 3. Tighten or "pull it snug" to the ring.

Lay the strand in place, up over the ring. This forms the first knotting stitch.

4. Make the second stitch with the lower raffia strand as shown in Figure 4. Loop the strand around the ring to the right of the first stitch, threading the raffia end through the loop and pulling it snug against the first stitch. Lay the strand in place, down over the ring. This forms the second knotting stitch.

Figure 3   *Figure 4*

5. As you follow this procedure, repeating Steps 3 and 4 all around the ring, you will see a pattern of the stitches beginning to form. One laps at the outer edge, the next laps at the inner edge. These stitches will be the base for attaching the first coil of needles.

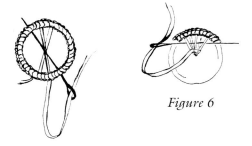

Figure 6

Figure 5

6. Split a length of raffia to a width of about 1/8", and thread it through the yarn needle. This will be used to form the spokes in the bottom of the ring.

Take a stitch through one of the loops formed by the knot on the inside rim of the ring, then bisect the ring across the center to make a spoke. Repeat to make a second spoke as shown in Figure 5.

7. Move the needle slightly to the left and come up to the left of the second spoke. Bisect the circle for the third spoke, and repeat to make a fourth spoke. Continue threading up to the left and down to the right until you have 16 or 20 evenly spaced spokes.

Finish the spokes by coming back to the center of the ring. Lay the raffia against another completed spoke, and tie a knot in the middle around all of the spokes. Push your needle through the center for firmness.

The spokes may be left as they are, or you may weave a design through them. If you choose not to weave, skip to step 9. When working with a 1" ring, weaving is a not necessary step, especially if you're a beginner.

8. The spokes may be woven, four at a time, working from the center out. (See Figure 6.) Slide your needle along a spoke, through the weave, to the center. Weave from right to left, going over the first, under the second, over the third, and under the fourth. Work back from the left to the right by going over the fourth, under the third, over the second, and under the first. Proceed around the ring, weaving four at a time, until the design is complete and the entire space is woven from the center to the rim.

Note: When you have only 2" or 3" of raffia left, end the strand by running it down a spoke and cutting it close to the weaving.

9. To begin coiling and stitching the basket bottom, select about six pine needles and hold them so that their ends taper in the same direction. The sheaths may be cut away (at an angle) if you don't want to include them in your design. Lay the needles against the edge of the ring, ends to the left, sheaths to the right. Stitch the first round through the knot stitches on the rim of the ring, sewing around the coil from front to back. Pull the stitches rather firmly to hold the coil in place.

10. In the second bottom coil, take each stitch through the corresponding stitch in the first round. At the same time, pass through part of the bundle at that point to give added security. Space the stitches evenly.

Figure 7

11. The third bottom coil, and all of the remaining coils in the basket bottom, are sewn with a double split stitch. Make the first half of the stitch by pushing your needle into the center of the stitch in the previous row, carrying the strand to one side over the bundle, and bringing your needle back through the center, starting point. Then carry the raffia strand to the other side over the bundle for the next half of the split stitch. See Figure 7. Stitch about one-third of the way through the second coil and begin the next stitch. As the basket increases in diameter, you can place new stitches at the midpoints between stitches previously made.

12. To start a new length of raffia, push your needle, threaded with the end of the first strand, down through a few rows and cut it off. Thread the new length, and bring it up through a few rows and out where you want to continue.

13. The basket sides are made by angling a coil on top of the last coil used for the base. Bring the ends of your pine needles from the base row up and make the first row of the sides. Stitch your rows as you did the base, at the vertical angle of your choice.

14. When the sides are as high as you'd like, and you want to finish off the basket, work to about 2" from the pine needle ends. Then cut the ends at an angle. Continue to stitch, taking the last few stitches through the previous row so that the ends blend into the rest of the basket.

15. To make the lid, coil and sew a flat disc of needles to fit the opening. (Alternatively, you can curve your disc to make a dome-shaped lid.) Sew a small pine cone in the center to serve as decoration and as a knob to lift the lid. Other small pine cones can be added to the sides, if desired, for handles.

16. As an optional step, you may shellac the basket to give it added durability. Use a brush and apply only pure, white shellac and denatured alcohol; other finishes may cause yellowing.

Gold Leaf Mirror

see photo page 98

Bay leaves, sometimes called laurel leaves, are prized worldwide for their aromatic flavor. Ancient Greeks honored achievement with laurel wreaths, and the true bay leaves that frame this mirror originate in Turkey.

This "gold leaf" mirror is covered with overlapping rows of Turkish bay leaves painted with gleaming acrylic gold. Tiny gilded peppercorns dotting the leaves give a textured dimension to the finish.

MATERIALS

    mirror, single thickness, 8" x 10"
    2 pieces of corrugated cardboard (strong),
        each 13" x 15"
    4–5 jars of Turkish bay leaves
    moss
    1 jar of peppercorns
    duct tape
    wood strip
    gold metallic craft paint
    1/4" x 2" wood strip, 13" long
    picture wire
    decorator ribbon (optional)

TOOLS

    sharp knife
    glue gun
    #5 or #6 paint brush
    staple gun

INSTRUCTIONS

1. Measure and cut (together) two cardboard pieces 13" x 15" (or 5" larger than your mirror dimensions).

2. Center and cut a rectangular frame opening measuring 7" x 9" (or 1" smaller than your mirror) in one piece of cardboard.

3. Using duct tape, attach the mirror (with a 1/4" overlap) firmly to the back (uncut) piece of cardboard. The tape must not show when the front frame is attached.

4. Glue the front cardboard frame to the back piece. Secure it firmly in place with ample glue

from your glue gun, and allow adequate drying time.

5. Glue the wood strip (about the size of a wood ruler) to the cardboard back about one-third of the distance down from the top edge. Let the glue dry thoroughly.

6. Attach a picture hanging wire to the wood piece using heavy-duty staples. Be careful not to apply any staples into the back of the glass mirror.

7. Lay the moss, gently mounded, around the entire front frame. Using the glue gun, attach the moss to the frame, pressing it firmly into place.

8. Lay out a large tray covered with paper towels, and gently pull the bay leaves out of their bottles onto the flat surface. Taking note of the larger leaves, lay out enough of the better shaped leaves to begin at the top center and save the best ones to finish at the bottom center.

9. Begin gluing the leaves into place; overlap them in rows going from top right to bottom center and from top left to bottom center. Fill in the rows with appropriate sizes (i.e., long, thin leaves at narrow edges, and fat, round leaves at the corners, etc.). Cover all of the moss mound around the frame.

10. At the top center, glue in about six leaves at cross angles, blending a fill-in leaf design to cover any openings at the beginning rows.

11. Glue peppercorns by twos on top of the leaves, at leaf points, and at other interesting locations. To add more texture, glue wildflowers, herbs, or berry plants onto the moss, using your own imagination and design.

12. When the frame has the design you like, brush gold paint over the entire surface. Let it dry completely before handling. An optional final step is to tie a decorator ribbon into a bow and attach it in one corner of the gilded frame.

Heart of Gold

see photo page 99

A warm sophistication makes this small heart of glittering gold a special gift, or an elegant welcome at your door. A double heart ring holding a generous thickness of moss is covered with layered rows of little bay leaves painted a metallic gold.

MATERIALS

> 8" (across) double-ring metal heart form
> moss
> bay leaves (in quantity)
> gold craft paint
> turpentine
> gold decorator ribbon

TOOLS

> glue gun
> #4 paint brush

INSTRUCTIONS

1. Press and glue the moss into a thick, lush mound over the entire surface of the metal heart form.

2. Shake the bay leaves out onto a flat surface.

3. Beginning at the center top of the moss-covered heart, glue and layer the bay leaves in rows from top to bottom. Choose compatible sizes of leaves to completely cover the moss.

4. Brush the leaves with gold paint and let them dry.

5. Attach the gold decorator ribbon by tying a simple knot and draping the ends as swags.

Rice Paper Pillow Sachet—
For a Scented Room

see photo page 100

Although it was called "rice paper" by the first Europeans and Americans to be introduced to it, this beautiful, translucent material is not made from rice, nor is it a true paper. Nevertheless, the misnomer persists to this day. In fact, it is a product of nature—the thin sheets of rice paper are cut spirally from the pith of the kung-shu tree that grows in the hills of northern Taiwan.

You will discover the delights of working with rice paper, with its delicate, swirling textured patterns, when you make these fragrant drawer sachets. A rice paper sachet filled with your very own potpourri adds a gentle scent to the bedroom and makes a very special gift.

Potpourri is easy to make, and it's nearly impossible to make a mistake. Start with dried flowers and leaves from your own garden, adding your own, homegrown herbs or some that you find in your local supermarket. You can create a potpourri for any mood or room just by varying the ingredients and their proportions. A recipe for a lavender potpourri is included in the instructions.

MATERIALS

> dried flowers, herbs, leaves, cones, spices, or whatever you want to use for your potpourri
> orrisroot powder
> essential oils
> 1 sheet of rice paper
> light cardboard
> white paper ribbon
> glue

TOOLS

> T-square
> #4 flat paint brush
> scissors
> ruler

INSTRUCTIONS
Making Potpourri

1. Select your flowers and herbs to make a

pleasing combination. Because this potpourri will be used for sachets, its scent is more important than its appearance. You can feel free to use flowers that are more harmonious in their fragrance than their color.

2. After you've blended all of the ingredients together, you need to add a fixative. This helps your potpourri continue to hold its scent. Orrisroot is the easiest fixative to find, and it takes on whatever scent you want. Add approximately one tablespoon for each cup of potpourri you make.

3. You can rely solely on the fragrance of your ingredients, or you can enhance the scent of your potpourri with one or more essential oils. For instance, you might use a single oil essence, like damask rose, or combine two or three to make whatever fragrance you like. All dried flowers, spices, and herbs contribute to the overall scent of the blend, but the essential oil is the most dominant.

4. Before you can use it, you must allow your potpourri to mature. Put your mixture into a large jar (a large canning jar works well), and put the jar where it won't be exposed to direct light. Except to stir the mixture daily, keep the jar sealed tightly for six weeks.

Making the Sachet
5. Measure and cut a 7" x 7" pattern from light cardboard.

6. Trace the square pattern onto the inside (wrong side) of the rice paper. Rice paper has definite front and back sides; the textured swirls are on the front, and the back is smooth. Trace two pieces for each sachet pillow you want to make. Cut the squares one at a time as needed.

7. Lay two of the 7" x 7" rice paper squares side by side, smooth side up.

8. Squeeze white tacky glue into a small, flat dish. Brush a 1" strip of glue 1" in from the outer edge on three sides of the bottom sheet. Make sure to leave one end open (no glue).

9. Turn the top sheet over so that the right, textured side faces up. Matching all of the edges, set the top sheet onto the bottom, glued sheet. Press all of the edges gently, but firmly together, and let the glue dry completely (20 to 30 minutes).

10. Gently pour 1/2 to 2/3 cup potpourri into the open side of the pillow, and allow the potpourri to fall to the bottom. Slowly lay the pillow down, being careful to keep the potpourri away from the opening. Then brush glue along the open side, 1" in from edge. Press the edges together firmly, and smooth the side. Allow the pillow to lay flat while the glue dries. Don't let the potpourri move around in the pillow until the glue is completely dry.

11. Cut a twisted white cord of paper ribbon into 9" strips. You'll need two for each sachet pillow.

12. Make a firm, tight knot in the center of the 9" paper ribbon piece. Check the length of the paper ribbon; it should reach across the square evenly on each side. You may have to trim the ends to fit. Glue the ribbon into place and let it dry. Optionally, you can make a bow trim by untwisting the ends of the 9" paper ribbon and carefully opening them into fans. Glue one paper bow on the front, and one on the back of your rice paper sachet pillow.

Recipe for Lavender Potpourri
1 cup pink rose petals

1/4 cup pink rose buds

1/2 cup lavender flowers

1/2 ounce rose geranium leaves

1/2 ounce blue delphinium blossoms

4 tablespoons orrisroot power

5 drops rose oil

2 drops lavender oil

Dry all of the flowers and leaves until they are crisp. Mix them together in a large bowl, and add the orrisroot powder. Mix well. Add the oils one drop at a time, mixing well after each drop. After placing the mixture in a jar, let it mature for six weeks. Stir daily while the potpourri is curing.

Tassels of Raffia and Gold Lamé

see photo page 101

A dictionary defines a tassel as "a bunch of loose threads or cords, bound at one end, hanging free from the other, to use as an ornament."

Here, the natural feel of raffia is blended with the glamorous sparkle of metallic gold. These decorative tassels can be used as an ornament for your Christmas tree, to enhance a wrapped package, or in any way that stirs your imagination.

MATERIALS

   25-30 strands of raffia, natural or colored, 7" long
   1 spool gold lamé thread
   4 strands of raffia (cord twist), 20" long
   waxed dental floss or other strong thread

TOOLS

   scissors
   yarn needle

INSTRUCTIONS

1. Grasp a bundle of 25 or 30 raffia strands, and cut them to 7". Cut ten to 15 pieces of gold lamé thread, each 7" long.

2. Gently spread out the raffia strands, and intermingle the lengths of gold thread. Gather all of the strands together as one bundle, and tie it firmly at the center with dental floss. (See Figure 1.)

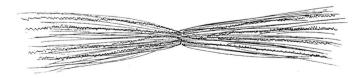

Figure 1

3. Measure and cut four "good" raffia strands, each 20" long, dampen, and lay them out straight.

4. Now twist two of the strands together firmly from one end to the other. Repeat with the other two strands. Then lay the twisted strands down, weight the ends, and let them dry.

5. Knot the twisted raffia strands together at one end, divide them in half (two strands together on each side), and slip the halves around the center tie. The first end-knot will stay at center underside of the bundle, and a second knot is tied on the top of the bundle. Now twist the four strands together into one cord.

3/4" down, tie with floss or thread.

Figure 2

6. Bend the ends of the tassel bundle downward from the center over the first knot, and tie the bundle 3/4" down from the top using dental floss. (See Figure 2.)

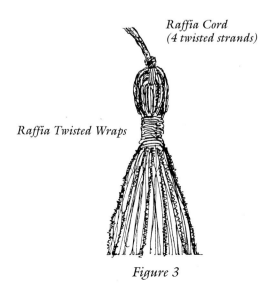

Raffia Cord (4 twisted strands)

Raffia Twisted Wraps

Figure 3

115

7. Thread one wider piece of raffia into a yarn needle. Lay the end of the raffia over the floss, and twist-wrap six to eight times firmly around the bundle (see Figure 3).

8. Working in reverse, knot the cord together with a second bundle of raffia to create a tassel on the other end of the cord.

9. Tie a center knot in the cord. Finished, the twisted raffia cord plus tassels should measure approximately 14".

10. Holding the tassel ends together in one hand, trim them with scissors, making all of the ends an even 3" long.

Holiday Reindeer Ornament

see photo page 102

Woven strips of split cattail leaves make this charming reindeer Christmas ornament. When cattail leaves are dry, they split easily along a straight line. Using a sharp knife, split the leaves lengthwise into strips 1/4" wide. You can usually get two, three, or four strips per leaf, depending on the leaf width.

Having found a stand of cattails, choose those with the stoutest stems, and cut the stems at their bases. Each stalk carries ten to 12 of the long, slim leaves. Cut a few having thin stems as well. Cutting two dozen or so stalks will assure you of an ample supply of material.

MATERIALS

> 5 strips of cattail leaves (per ornament)
> raffia
> potpourri (optional)
> glue (optional)

TOOLS

> scissors
> needle and thread

INSTRUCTIONS

1. To make one reindeer, you will need the following strip lengths:

strip 1	10"
strips 2 and 3	18"
strip 4	11"
strip 5	9"

Figure 1

2. Start with strip 1, and fold it in the shape shown in Figure 1. One end of this strip is one antler and the other end is the tail.

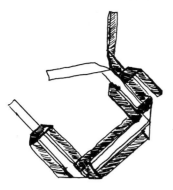

Figure 2

3. Now fold strip 2 around it as indicated. Strip 2 starts as the second antler, then winds back and forth to constitute part of the body, and finishes as part of the head. Be sure to thread the second strip under and over the first exactly as shown in Figure 2.

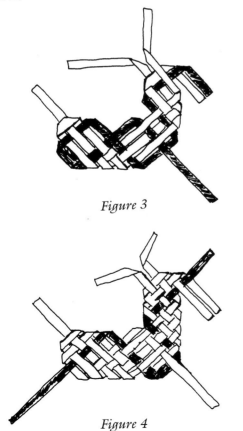

Figure 3

Figure 4

4. The diagrams show a loose weave in order to make the pattern clear, but in the actual construction, you must weave closely. Strips 3, 4, and 5 are folded and woven around the first two as indicated in the succeeding figures.

Figure 5

5. When all of the strips are in place, complete the head; turn under the pieces that end at the nose, and glue them in place if necessary. Cut the "hoof" ends on an angle, cut three tiny slits in the tail, and split the antler ends.

6. Complete the reindeer by providing a hanger: Braid three raffia strips into a 12" length. Tie the braid ends together and catch them with a needle and thread. Tease the braid ends into place in back of the reindeer's neck.

7. For a finishing touch, you might want to brush glue over your cattail reindeer and sprinkle on some of your favorite spice, herbal, or pine needle potpourri.

Sand Dollar Seashells—
For the Christmas Tree
see photo page 102

Part of the game of finding sand dollar shells for this Christmas project is knowing when and where to look! You'll need to head for the lagoons and sandy stretches along the seacoast where sand dollars abound. While the sand dollars in exposed coastal areas burrow beneath the sand, those in protected areas are often found two-thirds uncovered. Characteristically, the shells are found stuck in the sand at an angle, and low tide is the best time to gather a bagful.

You will need approximately 30 to 40 of these thin, circular shells to decorate a medium-sized Christmas tree. Plan to gather some extras, allowing for those that might chip or crack in the crafting process.

MATERIALS

> sand dollars
> chlorine bleach
> white acrylic paint
> 1/2"-wide satin ribbon
> red berry wire
> ornament hooks

TOOLS

> drill with 1/16" or 1/32" bit
> craft knife (optional)
> scissors
> flat paint brush

INSTRUCTIONS

1. Mix a two-to-one solution of chlorine bleach and water, and soak the shells overnight. Bleaching the shells will completely remove any lingering odor and will loosen barnacles. If barnacles still adhere to the shells after soaking, scrape them away. Bleaching will also whiten their natural gray color. Boiling is another widely used method of cleaning the shells (though some collectors feel that boiling fades the color of a shell).

2. Using an electric drill with the smallest drill bit (1/16" or 1/32"), you can drill holes approximately 3/4" from the edge (not too close to the edge, or the shell may chip).

Another way to make a hole in a seashell is to hold the tip of a craft knife upright where you want the hole to be, and while applying steady pressure, twist the tip of the blade until a hole is cut through the shell. Using the knife method gives you more control, and the shell is less likely to break.

3. Drill where you won't distort the figure on the upper surface of the sand dollar. This figure looks like a flower with five petals, and the area above the two shorter "petals" is an ideal place to drill a hole.

4. Sand dollar shells are very porous; therefore, two coats of white acrylic paint (brushed or sprayed) will be needed to attain an attractive, smooth white surface. Two coats of paint on each shell will prevent the shell from fading and will not darken the shell. Shellac is particularly prone to discoloration on sand dollars.

Apply the first coat of paint and let it dry thoroughly. This is easily absorbed by the shell. Put the second coat on sparingly, so you won't paint out the natural petal design on the upper part of the shell. Use a white acrylic "wet look" paint, or a white enamel-like paint.

5. Thread a 12" length of 1/2"-wide satin ribbon through each drilled hole, and tie it into a bow. Then slip one piece of red berry wire (available in packets of 20 in craft shops) through the knot of the bow. Finally, insert the small end of an ornament hook up through the drilled hole under the ribbon.

6. Many other decorative combinations can also be used on the sand dollars. Try adding a bit of lace, some moss, or dried flowers to your satin ribbon bow. Signed and wrapped in tissue, a sand dollar tree ornament makes a very special gift to send in the Christmas box!

Pine Cone Basket Ornament

see photo page 104

Woven of natural reed, this beautiful bit of basketry becomes a cherished ornament to hang on the Christmas tree year after year. Even if you have never made a basket before, you can create this delicate basket ornament in just one evening. Fill it with tiny pine cones and berry sprigs or, for some added fragrance, pieces of cinnamon stick, dried citrus peels, and cloves.

MATERIALS

1 coil of #1.5 reed
ribbon
miniature pine cones
pepper berries or other red berries
plastic bag
rubber band
soft fiber fill

TOOLS

scissors
ruler

INSTRUCTIONS

1. Cut four 60", four 20", and one 20" lengths of reed from your coil. Soak them in lukewarm water until they're flexible.

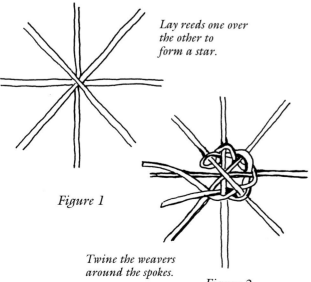

Lay reeds one over the other to form a star.

Figure 1

Twine the weavers around the spokes.

Figure 2

2. Cross the four 20" lengths to make spokes as shown in Figure 1. Gently bend one of the 60" lengths in half and slip the center loop around one spoke for a weaver. Mentally label the half in front of the spoke "A" and the half behind the spoke "B." Twine to the right, crossing weaver "A" over weaver "B," and continue the over and under pattern (see Figure 2).

3. Continue twining for twelve rounds. Hold the basket in one hand and shape it into a bowl, pressing the weave close. End the weaver by cutting and twining it behind a spoke, and pushing the ends in to blend with the weave. Set it aside.

4. Stuff a wad of fiberfill (any cotton-like soft fill) about the size of a tennis ball into the plastic bag and secure it with a bag tie. Insert the ball form into the partially woven ornament, and gently bend the reeds around the soft ball to form the ornament's egg shape.

5. Repeat Step 3 to weave the top half of the ornament beginning above the plastic bag of polyester fiberfill. Use the remaining 60" reed, and weave until the ornament is 5–6" high.

6. Grasp the spokes together at the top of the ornament with two fingers and cut the ends even, approximately 1" beyond the grasp. Bend the reed ends over 1" and secure them with the rubber band.

7. Snip an opening in the plastic bag, and carefully remove the stuffing and the bag.

8. Use a wet towel to moisten the banded ends or soak the ends briefly in water if necessary. From the 24" length, cut a 4" piece for a hanger. Bend the hanger loop piece over the banded spokes. With the remainder of the length, wrap the handle and banded spokes as one unit. Wrap evenly and firmly. Finish by inserting the end into the weave of the ornament.

9. Tie the red ribbon around the wrapped spokes and finish with a bow at the top.

Glass Ball Tree Ornament

see photo page 103

Potpourri literally translated from the French means "rotten pot"; originally, flowers and spices were layered with salt in a crock to ferment them, preserving a long-lasting scent. During the 16th century, finished mixtures became more widely available and were kept in bowls to sweeten the air of small homes. By the 18th century, many recipes for potpourri had been written and handed down through generations.

Although no two of these glass ornaments are exactly alike, they all share the sweet smells of Christmas. Each clear glass ball seems not only to reflect but to generate light from its colorful mix of potpourri deep inside.

Each glass ball is individually filled by hand with a Christmas mix of potpourri and tied with the fanciest taffeta ribbon. A subtle variety of potpourri scents promises to make Christmas a happy memory.

MATERIALS

> clear glass ball ornaments
> potpourri, Christmas mix with pine cones
>   and flowers, or other
> 2"-wide, gold trimmed, taffeta decorator
>   ribbon (burgundy, dark red, pink)
> ornament hanger

TOOLS

> tweezers
> glue gun

INSTRUCTIONS

1. Add cinnamon stick pieces, tiny pine cones, crumbled bay leaves, nutmeg, and cloves (soak the cloves in essence of orange oil before using them) to a basic potpourri recipe, or purchase a Christmas mix.

2. Remove the gold foil caps from the glass ornaments, and place them in special container for safe keeping.

3. Put several varieties of potpourri and spices (cinnamon, nutmeg, cloves, etc.) into individual bowls.

4. Place a clear glass ornament on a white towel in front of you (glass ball ornaments can roll away easily). Using your tweezers, begin filling the glass ball with one variety of potpourri petals and spices until the ball is filled to the top. The potpourri in the glass ball should cover the metal spring clamps of the gold cap.

5. Cut a piece of ribbon 18" long, and make a simple bow to glue onto the top of the ornament. Bend the wire edges of the bow and ends to make an attractive shape.

6. Replace the gold foil cap on the ornament, and glue the bow to the top of the ornament directly over the gold foil cap. Let it dry before hanging the ornament on the tree.

Sugar Cone Ornaments
With "Chocolate" Pine Cone Topping and "Vanilla" Flower Topping

see photo page 103

Part of the Christmas magic is decorating the tree. A tempting sugar cone ornament filled with "pine cone chocolate" and "flower-flavored vanilla" captures this magical spirit for sure! All ages will delight in transforming the familiar ice cream sugar cone into an enchanting Christmas tree ornament.

Wandering through the woods to gather a collection of tiny cedar cones (or miniature pine cones) is great fun for kids as well as grown-ups. Dried, pale-colored flowers from your garden evoke memories of the summer's bounty. Use your assortment to "flavor" some ornaments for the Christmas tree, the holiday bazaar, and the Christmas party too.

These sugar cone ornaments are sturdy favorites and will last and last through many Christmases.

MATERIALS

> sugar cones with 5" wide wrap
> rigid plastic foam balls, each 2-1/4" diameter
> dried flowers and leaves (straw flowers, globe flowers, statice, white or white and pink mix)
> small tree cones (pine or cedar)
> red pepper berry
> polyurethane spray
> gold cord, 6" long for each ornament
> glue
> straight pins

TOOLS

> tweezers
> glue gun

INSTRUCTIONS

1. Holding one sugar cone in your hand, apply a 1/2" band of glue around the inside top edge. Place the foam ball firmly but gently onto the cone and let the glue dry.

2. Begin decorating the cone and ball with a 5" length of your gold cord. Pin the two ends of the cord close together at the center top of the plastic foam ball.

3. Using tweezers, pick up one pine cone (or tiny blossom), apply glue to the bottom with the glue gun, and press the pine cone (or blossom) tightly and firmly onto the rigid plastic foam ball. Continue until the ball is completely covered, gluing and pressing the pine cones (or flowers) as close together as possible. The topping should be the heaviest where it meets the edges of the cone, producing a large, round "ice cream scoop" look. You can enhance this effect by using slightly larger cones (or blossoms) at the edge of the sugar cone. Be generous with your topping; a thin covering gives the plastic foam ball a "bald" look.

4. Arrange the topping so that the ends of the gold cord at the top of the ball are hidden from view.

5. Spray the sugar cone lightly with polyurethane, and your sugar cone Christmas ornaments will last indefinitely.

NATURE CRAFT BASICS

Gathering the ingredients for your nature craft projects is often more than half the fun. A walk through the woods, a stroll along the beach, or a tour of some marshlands can be a journey of discovery. It is a time to notice small details, to breathe nature's aromas, and to find things of beauty to bring home as lasting mementos. Let's explore together some of the many materials available, and how they can be used for craft projects.

VINES

Vines—nature's rope—grow almost everywhere, but they are especially prevalent along the heavily wooded banks of rivers and streams. Although they're a bit knobby where the tendrils branch, vines are exceptionally strong and make fascinating baskets and wreaths. Not only are vines beautiful to work with, but they're usually growing in a spot where they need to be cut back and are free for the asking!

Pull on your hiking boots, and head for a likely wooded area. Vines can be cut all year long, but fall and winter, after the growing season has finished, are the best times to gather the long, flexible vines from woods and thickets. When you find your patch, scuff the toe of your boot under the vine, lift, take hold of the vine, and pull!

The year-old runners, only a few feet long, are best. Running the vines through a gloved hand, strip off the leaves. Coil the vines as you collect them so that they will fit into a big kitchen pot at home. Boiling is needed to make them pliable and keep them from shrinking after they have been shaped.

Back in your kitchen, push the coil into a cooking pot, and fill the pot with enough water to cover the vines. After boiling, cool; then pour off the water and drain. To retain the bark, which results in darker, woodsy-looking vines, boil them for just one hour. Vines boiled for two or three hours readily give up their coat. By running a gloved hand down these vines, you can easily remove the bark, leaving white, waxy-looking vines.

You can coil, dry, and store the boiled vines. Before you intend to use them, soak them for five or ten minutes to restore their resiliency.

Honeysuckle

Pretty and fragrant, yet exceptionally strong, honeysuckle vines are a joy to fashion into such delightful ephemera as Valentine's Day heart wreaths, and into such long-useful objects as small woven baskets. Look for honeysuckle in woods and thickets and along forest edges.

Grapevines

With their twisting tendrils, grapevines are always an effective conversation piece. They are not generally used for small, delicate projects, but they make a wonderful wreath for a 30"-wide door. Grapevines are often used indoors for wreaths placed over a fireplace mantle or for a dramatic basket on the dining room buffet.

Bittersweet

If you collect wild bittersweet in the fall, make sure to collect the vines too, as they are wonderfully flexible. The best ones are branches cut from the main vine that are at least a few feet long, and with a diameter ranging from 1/4" to 3/8". Strip the vine of berries and leaves to make wreaths 8" to 10" in diameter.

Wisteria

Wisteria is a very aggressive plant, but be careful to cut only the secondary runners, not the thick main trunk vine. These secondary vines grow back quickly after cutting. Strip the leaves, and coil the vines into a wreath shape to dry.

CATTAILS

Cattails, also known as bulrushes, are tall, graceful, reedy plants with brown flower heads. Look for cattails near the edges of ponds and in marshes. These tough plants can be found over a wider range of climates than most fibrous weaving materials, and are usually free for the asking.

Cut green cattail leaves at their height of growth between May and December. Lay them flat to dry; that prevents any shrinkage after your basket (or other project) is done. Re-dampen them for ease in weaving.

WILLOW WHIPS

Use whips—freshly cut, if possible—from the new sprouts of "creek willow" growing near water. Sprouts emerging from a clear-cut area, or the new shoots of pussy willow also work well, especially for basketry. Choose the least tapered stems to cut. Then, by running your hand from the tip to the base, strip away the leaves. The whips are now ready for weaving.

Willow whips that have dried thoroughly never completely regain their fresh-cut pliability, even when soaked in water. It is possible to keep whips pliable for several days after cutting them by immediately wrapping them in wet paper, leaves, or cloth, or by standing them in a tall bucket of water.

ROUND REED

Reed comes from the core of the rattan palm, a tropical, climbing plant with thorny shoots that can grow to a height of 500 feet. The inner pulp of these shoots consists of long fibers. Round reed is available in thicknesses from #00 to #10 (see Figure 1). Round reed is sold in hanks or bundles and is available in most craft shops.

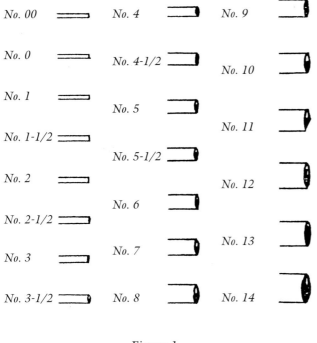

No. 00   No. 4   No. 9

No. 0   No. 4-1/2   No. 10

No. 1   No. 5

No. 1-1/2   No. 11

No. 5-1/2

No. 2   No. 12

No. 6

No. 2-1/2

No. 13

No. 3   No. 7

No. 3-1/2   No. 8   No. 14

Figure 1
Reed Sizes

Reed must be dampened well before you work with it, or it will break (#2 reed should be left in the bath at least five minutes before it is supple enough to work with), and you must re-dampen it as soon as it begins to feel dry. Soak only the amount of reed you will be using shortly because the reed will fray if it is left too long in the water.

WOOD

Although your choice of wood for any rustic twig project will depend on the style of the piece and whether it is to be used indoors or out, here are some helpful suggestions:
• Rhododendron and laurel are highly durable and easy to work.
• Hickory is very flexible while it's green, has great strength, and its bark will survive considerable weathering.
• White oak and ash have bending properties similar to those of hickory.
• Red oak, birch, swamp dogwood, and some conifers are fairly durable outdoors.
• Elm has good flexibility and some interesting limb configurations but is impossible to cleave; furthermore, it will rot quickly if subjected to alternately wet and dry conditions.
• Willow is bendable and light but requires sturdy bracing.

• Hazel and shrublike red maple have bending properties similar to willow, and they are stronger than willow but not as durable outdoors.
• Splints for weaving chair seats and backs can be made from white oak, ash, and hickory.
• Fretwork panels and small twigs for bracing or for decoration are ideally taken from fruit tree prunings, holly, boxwood, or from an endless variety of hardwood twigs and tree roots.

SEASHELLS

Picking up shells as you walk barefoot on the beach, feeling the soft sea breezes, will always bring serenity and a fascination with nature's unlimited variety. In shells, you'll find perfect designs in pale pink and satiny white, and discover a myriad of shapes and patterns.

"Beach shells" are the empty shells left behind when the animal dies naturally; they are scattered on the sand in abundance as the tide ebbs. The best time for combing the beach is at low tide, especially after a storm. The turbulence of storm-driven waves can churn up the most interesting deposits. Because the shore line is constantly changing, you can explore the same area over and over again, and always find something new.

If you are land-bound, don't despair. Every shell imaginable is available from shell shops and mail-order houses. For the sake of the animals, and to assure a selection of shells for future beachcombers, always try to purchase shells that were not harvested live.

Cleaning Shells
Shells that are stained can be cleaned with linseed oil to restore the luster. Bleaching is only used to remove any lasting odor. Sand dollar shells are sometimes bleached (mix a half-and-half solution of bleach and water) to whiten their natural gray color. Soak them no more than thirty minutes, or you can weaken the shell. Soak small shells in an alcohol solution of four parts rubbing alcohol to one part water.

Drilling Shells
You can drill holes in shells by using an electric drill with the smallest drill bit (1/16" or 1/32"). Don't drill too close to the edges, or you may break the shell. To avoid chipping the surface, drill from the inside.

Another way to make a hole in a seashell is to hold the tip of a craft knife upright where you want the hole to be. Applying steady pressure, twist the tip of the blade until a hole is cut through the shell. Using the knife method you have more control, and the shell is less likely to break.

Polishing Shells

Acrylic craft spray is sometimes sprayed on shells displayed outdoors to keep them from fading. Shellac discolors sand dollars and other white shells.

DRYING FLOWERS

During the height of their blooming period, it is difficult to imagine that the beauty of fresh flowers will fade with the onset of shorter days and cooler weather. To preserve their beauty, and to use them for crafts throughout the year, flower blossoms and delicate greenery can be dried by a variety of methods.

Oven drying is a quick way to dry plants. If you want to dry just a few flowers quickly, follow these easy steps:

1. Arrange the flowers one layer deep on a cookie sheet.

2. Place them in a cool (100° F) oven with the door open slightly.

3. Watch the flowers carefully to make sure they don't become overcooked.

4. Oven drying can take from a few minutes to a few hours, depending on the moisture content of your material.

Hang drying is probably the easiest method to use for drying your own leaves, herbs, and flowers. Dry all greenery with the stems intact (these are ideal for bouquets and flower arrangements). In fact, leave the stems as long as possible on either flowers or leaves. If you are drying flowers, strip all of the leaves from the stems. Then follow these steps:

1. Bunch three to five stems together (the bigger the bunch, the longer it takes to dry), and secure them with a rubber band about 1" from the tips. The rubber band can also serve as hook to hang the flowers for drying.

2. Suspend the flowers with the blossoms facing down. Use a drying rack or multiple hangers on a clothes line.

3. Dry the flowers about a week until they are crisp, not tacky to the touch. Check them daily as they are drying.

For cultivated flowers such as pink globe flowers, larkspur, and lavender, the hang-dry method works especially well. Flower heads and petals can be removed from the stems after drying (for decorating, potpourris, and sachets).

MAKING WREATHS

The basic wreath is made with woodvine or grapevine, both of which are easy to gather and shape throughout the summer and into the fall (by late winter, they become too brittle to cooperate). The knobs, bends, and twists of the vine give the wreath its intriguing shape; they also create pockets in which you can place small plants for live greenery, or seasonal decorations such as dried flowers and fall leaves.

Head for the woods with your sharp clippers in hand, and find a suitable vine. One having interesting twists and irregularities is ideal. Pull and tug until you free three pieces several feet long, all having a diameter of 1" to 1-1/2". You will need a little extra length in order to choose the best sections of vine for making your wreath.

Figure 2

Starting with one long, thick length of vine, cross the ends over one another to form a circle the size you want. Grasping the crossover point with one hand, use your other hand to pull one end of the vine through the middle of the circle. Wrap it around to the outside and up through the center again. You are making long spirals with it. (See Figure 2.) Repeat this wrapping procedure with the other end of the vine. Secure the ends by simply tucking them into the twists of the vine.

You'll find that heavy vine an inch or more in diameter will only pull through your circle two or three times. Vines of a smaller diameter will wrap more tightly and can be used to make a smaller wreath, or to fill in the center of a wreath started with the thicker vine.

WEAVING BASKETS

Weaving a basket is easy, and the possibilities are endless for making baskets using nature's materials.

Basketry materials have two major functions: the vertical elements, called "stakes," form the skeleton of a basket; the horizontals, called "weavers," weave over and under the stakes to make the basket's walls.

Some of the more familiar weaving terms that you will find in these projects include the following:

Breaking Down: Dividing one group of stakes into more than one smaller groups. For example, taking paired stakes and dividing them into singles, making twice the original number of stakes.

Bye-stake: A stake added to the total to make an odd number of stakes.

Center: The first few rounds of weaving that bind the stakes together.

Coil: One round of weaving.

Stakes: The elements used for the frame of the basket—the verticals; they are held together and filled in by the weavers.

Weavers: The elements used for weaving over and under the stakes to make the walls of the basket—the horizontals.

Upsett: The point at which the stakes are bent upward (usually to make the sides of the basket).

To make a basket, you always begin at the bottom. Using a woven base to start, you proceed up the sides of the basket, finishing off with the top, (or outer) border. The stakes bend back to form the border, locking the weavers and holding the basket together.

Twining a Basket

1. Gently bend a length of reed (or other weaver) in half, and slip the loop around one of the stakes. Mark the end of the stake with an "X" to identify it as the starting point.

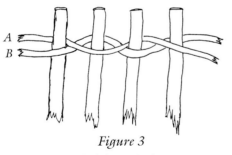

Figure 3

Twining a Basket

2. Mentally label the reed half in back of the stake "A," and the half in front of the stake "B." Working to the right, bring weaver "A" over weaver "B," in front of the next stake. Then pass weaver "B" under weaver "A," behind the second stake, and out to the front. Repeat the twining motion around all of the stakes. (See Figure 3.)

3. When your weaver runs short before your project is finished, lay a new piece alongside the old one, letting the new weaver cross in front of the old one. Join the pieces behind a stake or pair of stakes, and leave the remaining ends resting against a stake. Trim the ends when the work is finished.

For a Scalloped Border

This is the simplest kind of border. First, make sure all of the upright stakes are trimmed off to the same length. Next, poke a knitting needle or awl down alongside one stake. Insert the end of the next closest stake about 2" into the weaving (see Figure 4). Repeat with each spoke in turn.

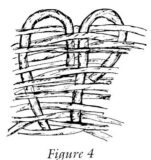

Figure 4

A Scalloped Border

For a Soft Rim

Start by cutting off the spokes just above the weaving. Then make a bundle of flat elements like cattail leaves or thin bamboo slices to use for the rim. Thread a needle with raffia, strong grass, or a narrow braid of cattail leaves, and, holding the bundle atop the raw edge, whipstitch the bundle to the top edge of the basket. Stitch all the way around in one direction; then reverse the direction of your stitches to make a very firm, finished border (see Figure 5).

Figure 5

A Soft Rim

Helpful Hints for Making Baskets

• An uneven number of stakes is necessary when using a single weaver, or you'll weave over and under the same stakes in every row.

• If you are right handed, weave from left to right. If you are left handed, weave from right to left.

• Think of weaving as "laying in" the weaver between the stakes, where each "laying in" fixes the shape. Avoid pulling the weaver. Instead, push the reed coils close together to alleviate any gaps between rows.

APPENDIX

DIMENSIONS FOR BIRDHOUSES

SPECIES	Floor of cavity	Depth of cavity	Entrance above floor	Diameter of entrance	Height above ground
	Inches	Inches	Inches	Inches	Feet
Bluebird	5 x 5	8	6	1-1/2	5–10
Robin	6 x 8	8	(1)	(1)	6–15
Chickadee	4 x 4	8–10	6–8	1-1/8	6–15
Titmouse	4 x 4	8–10	6–8	1-1/4	6–15
Nuthatch	4 x 4	8–10	6–8	1-1/4	12–20
House wren	4 x 4	6–8	1–6	1	6–10
Carolina wren	4 x 4	6–8	1–6	1-1/8	6–10
Tree swallow	5 x 5	6	1–5	1-1/2	10–15
Barn swallow	6 x 6	6	(1)	(1)	8–12
Purple martin	6 x 6	6	1	2-1/2	15–20
Song sparrow	6 x 6	6	(2)	(2)	1–3
House finch	6 x 6	6	4	2	8–12
Phoebe	6 x 6	6	(1)	(1)	8–12
Crested flycatcher	6 x 6	6–10	6–8	2	8–20
Flicker	7 x 7	16–18	14–16	2-1/2	6–20
Red-headed woodpecker	6 x 6	12–15	9–12	2	12–20
Downy woodpecker	4 x 4	8–10	6–8	1-1/4	6–20
Hairy woodpecker	6 x 6	12–15	9–12	1-1/2	12–20

(1) One or more sides open   (2) All sides open

Chart courtesy of "Homes For Birds," Farmer's Bulletin #1456.

INDEX

METRIC CONVERSION CHART	
INCHES	CM
1/8	0.3
1/4	0.6
3/8	1.0
1/2	1.3
5/8	1.6
3/4	1.9
7/8	2.2
1	2.5
1-1/4	3.2
1-1/2	3.8
1-3/4	4.4
2	5.1
2-1/2	6.4
3	7.6
3-1/2	8.9
4	10.2
4-1/2	11.4
5	12.7
6	15.2
7	17.8
8	20.3
9	22.9
10	25.4
11	27.9
12	30.5
13	33.0
14	35.6
15	38.1
16	40.6
17	43.2
18	45.7
19	48.3
20	50.8

ACKNOWLEDGEMENTS

To my "northwoods" father, Irving Cook, for his lifelong love of woods, streams, and wilderness. His gentle, adventurous spirit of discovery remains undiminished in my memory, and I am deeply grateful.

To my husband, Bill, whose countless hours of patient designing and building made my many wood craft ideas take wing, a profound and appreciative thank you.

To my editor Leslie Dierks, for her suggestions, guidance, and good-natured support, my gratitude.

Finally, with admiration to Rob Pulleyn, who tastefully published my very first projects in magazine articles, and has carefully guided the production of this book, I am extremely grateful.